THE BIBLE AND COUNSELLING

23rd July   Herbie

By the same author

Understanding Adolescence
Coping with Illness
Roots & Shoots

THE BIBLE
AND
COUNSELLING

ROGER HURDING

Hodder & Stoughton
LONDON SYDNEY AUCKLAND

Copyright © 1992 by Roger Hurding

First published in Great Britain in 1992

The right of Roger Hurding to be identified as the Author of
the Work has been asserted by him in accordance with the
Copyright, Designs and Patents Act 1988.

10 9 8 7 6 5

British Library Cataloguing in Publication Data
A record for this book is available from the British Library

ISBN 0 340 51742 5

Printed and bound in Great Britain by
Cox & Wyman Ltd, Reading, Berkshire

Hodder and Stoughton
A Division of Hodder Headline PLC
338 Euston Road
London NW1 3BH

To friends and colleagues
at
NETWORK

Diagrams

Contents

Preface

Two days before I was due to start writing this book I slipped a disc. The occasion was New Year's Eve 1988. A few months before, Joy and I had just recovered from a period of illness, my own general health had improved remarkably over the intervening weeks, I was looking forward to a fresh bout of writing and keenly anticipated an evening of celebration. The last party game we played that night was not particularly demanding on wit, wind or limb (or so I thought at the time) and included the growth of a crocodile of people, winding through the house. My limited vision and stumbling gait (both complications of longstanding diabetes) necessitated a pretty firm grip on the person in front of me. Unfortunately, she was not the tallest at the party and our hilarious stampeding through the house exposed an old weakness in my back. Thirty-six hours later I was prostrated with pain.

For most of 1989 I was unable to touch the typewriter, although a spinal operation in May led to gradual improvement by the end of the year. However, at that stage the cataract in my one sighted eye needed surgery. This operation, early in 1990, was successful but, once more, there were many months when systematic writing was impossible. Within this period of convalescence, some of the same group of friends who had roared rumbustiously through the house on that fateful New Year's Eve clubbed together and bought the personal computer that I am now using. And so, this book, so elusive in the starting, has been the result of my new relationship with advanced technology. Growing fitfully in the computer's womb over the past year, the product, long overdue, has reached the time of public announcement and exposure to the gaze of others.

I suppose the closest watchers of this particular pregnancy are my friends and colleagues at Network, a Christian counselling centre based in Bristol and founded in 1986. Prior to this date, I was one of a steering committee which prayed, debated and agonised over the basis, aims and methods of Network. From the beginning, we were keen that the organisation held three perspectives in harmony and equal importance: the offer of a counselling service to supplement and support the caring work of local churches; the availability of a resource centre which would help identify and encourage co-operation within the existing network of caring in the community; and the initiation of training programmes, both to help Christians be more effective listeners and carers and to train counsellors for Network and elsewhere. One day, in the summer of 1985, I had the temerity to offer a detailed proposal for a training scheme for Network. This was 'unanimously welcomed' by the Council of Management, and in the autumn of that year we began the first of our training courses. The basis of my thinking and planning for the original scheme (including material I had used at Trinity College, Bristol) has evolved into our current Introductory and Main Courses which, together, occupy an academic year. *The Bible and Counselling* is the product of all this groundwork.

Why this particular book? Apart from its growth from a background of training Christians to be more effective carers, it is written to try to encourage the many who long to help others in the name of Christ but, somehow, are often frustrated as to how they can link their understanding of the Bible with their listening and counselling. Some feel obliged to quote biblical texts to (or, more problematically, *at*) those who seek the way forward. Sometimes, they find, this method leads to constructive change and growth. At other times, the approach seems to distance the one who comes for help. Others, perhaps made cautious by having been on the receiving end of a heavy-handed use of Scripture, bend over backwards to avoid any mention to their clients of the book they love and study. There are other Christians who simply do not see any direct link between the Bible (whose trustworthiness they may question anyway) and their caring and counselling. Further, a great number of believers work in the caring professions and secular counselling organisations and feel constrained *not* to use the Scriptures openly in their work, for fear of taking advantage of their clients and patients. Their diffidence may arise from organisational policy for carers to avoid declaring their own world-views or from a natural reluctance to capitalise on the vulnerability of people in their neediest hour. It is dilemmas like these that *The Bible and Counselling* aims to uncover, discuss and find ways of resolving.

The following pages can be used in any of three main ways. They may form the basis of private study and act as a stimulus for increased self-understanding and growth in Christian maturity. To this end, each chapter concludes with a 'personal reflection'. Secondly, the book could be valuable for any gathering of Christians who decide to meet on a regular basis, using the 'group discussion' material suggested, again at the end of each chapter. Thirdly, *The Bible and Counselling* can be used as the foundation for training schemes in caring and counselling – within local churches, at residential study-centres, by Christian counselling organisations or other bodies committed to the caring ministries.

I am grateful to friends at Network who have, in turn, encouraged, tolerated and been frustrated by my various enthusiasms and projects. As well as their general affirmation, they have been remarkably patient with the vagaries of my illnesses – not least when, at the end of the first pilot year of training, my sudden unavailability put a great deal on to the capable shoulders of the then new director, John Turner. The names of valued colleagues are too numerous to mention fully but let me record a special thanks to those most involved with the development of the training. They include the first two directors of Network, David Mitchell and John Turner, as well as Tim Hockridge, Paul Main, Christine Mitchell, Julia Patterson, Alison Sankey and Anne Turner.

My sincerest thanks are due to the many patients and clients who have shared their stories with me through the past thirty years or so. Although I have included ingredients of some of these stories within this book, confidentiality has been respected and identifiable details have been altered accordingly. Further, I am indebted once more to my different editors, especially to David Wavre, Christine Plunkett, Carolyn Armitage and Bryony Bénier, who have variously offered advice and comment through the somewhat spasmodic stages of this book's gestation and delivery. Joy, as always, has been an invaluable co-labourer, supportive and patient over my alternating excitement and uncertainty as the book has taken shape.

Roger Hurding

1

The Bible: Blueprint for Counselling?

The Bible is alive, it speaks to me; it has feet, it runs after me; it has hands, it lays hold on me.

Martin Luther

Kate was in her early thirties when she first came to see me. My first impression was of a smiling and friendly manner, belied to some extent by a sad and suspicious expression in her eyes. She had come, somewhat reluctantly, through the recommendation of a friend and sought help for recurring feelings of inadequacy and self-dislike. As I listened to her story over the following weeks, she became more relaxed, smiled less automatically and, at times, came near to tears.

Her father was an authoritarian figure who had always favoured her talented older sister, Sonia, and given her the cream of his affection and interest. Whatever Sonia touched, she seemed to excel in – swimming for the prestigious school she had attended, playing the cello in the county's Youth Orchestra, achieving academically at university, marrying a gifted and personable lawyer and producing two beautiful children. Kate was clearly fond of her sister and yet expressed a deep inner sadness as she talked about her family.

She admitted that her mother had tried to compensate for her father's favouritism, but Kate had never felt really valued by either of her parents. She still had vivid memories of her father shouting at her when she became stuck with her homework and recalled some of his phrases that still rankled: 'Why can't you take a leaf out of your sister's book?', 'You know what you are? You're pathetic!' and, worst of all, 'I sometimes wonder where you came from!'. Kate's only weapon against this onslaught seemed to be a retreat into herself, a self that she came to see as not only bruised but of a nature which warranted that bruising from others. She admitted that she must have come across as a sullen and resentful child.

From her teen years onwards she learned to cope by presenting a smiling exterior and was seen as dependable, though somewhat aloof, in several secretarial jobs she undertook through her twenties. During this time, through a Christian friend's prayers and interest she began to commit herself, albeit tentatively, to Christ. However, the teaching she heard from the local church never seemed to penetrate the defensive layers that had been built up over her inner hurt.

In our discussions, Kate admitted to difficulty in relating to the opposite sex: she treated younger men with suspicion and older men with fear. Further, her powerful sense that fatherhood meant 'being criticised, undervalued and judged' had blocked her response to Christian talk of a heavenly Father.

It was only as she allowed her true feelings to surface and, in time, cried the tears she needed to cry, that the extent of her buried anger became clear. Although she was angry with her father, behind that burned a deep rage towards God. What could the Bible have to say, if anything, that would help Kate? As we talked about her negative feelings and the sense of guilt they aroused, it occurred to me to say, 'Do you know, Kate, God wants you to be angry with him!'. I had recently been reflecting on some of the Psalms in which the psalmist expresses his complaint, at what God seems to be doing or allowing, in the strongest terms. In fact, as I pointed out to Kate, although most of the Psalms of Lament close with some reassurance or vow to praise, one of them, Psalm 88, finishes with these bleak words:

> You have taken my companions
> and loved ones from me;
> the darkness is my closest friend. (v. 18)

This declaration might have seemed to offer little comfort to Kate, but it was just what was required. She needed permission from God himself to complain to him, to give vent to her anger, to tell him how she really felt, to ask for forgiveness and for the strength to forgive her father. As we prayed together, she found solace from the One who himself had cried, quoting another Psalm of Lament, 'My God, my God, why have you forsaken me?' (Mark 15:34).

As the story of Kate shows, the relationship between counselling and the Bible may be far from straightforward. It seemed right, at the appropriate stage, to point her to Psalm 88 and then to share something of Christ's experience of dereliction as described in the Gospels. Would my approach have been any less 'biblical' if I had continued to listen to and care for her without quoting from Scripture? What does it mean to be true to the Bible in our reaching out to others in need?

Christian circles bristle with approaches to counselling that lay claim to the Bible. They include many whose names suggest a measure of confidence about that claim: some emphasise a call to commitment, such as 'discipleship' counselling; others the method used, as in 'nouthetic' or 'prayer' counselling; while a number proclaim something more definitive, as with 'spiritual', 'Christian' or, most sweepingly, 'biblical' counselling.

It is the purpose of this chapter to explore just what we mean when we declare our approach to caring for others to be *biblical*. Does it simply show that we take the Scriptures seriously? Does it imply that we actively use the Bible in our counselling method, as I eventually did with Kate? Does it indicate that we believe that *every* aspect of our care, including assumptions, aims and techniques, is modelled on scriptural principles? If so, is that too big a claim for any- one to make? Is the word of God not too comprehensive, mysterious and profound for us to imply that we have it pigeon- holed?

In order to discover what it might mean for us to be true to the Scriptures in our caring and counselling, I suggest we address two main questions at this stage: How are we to view the Bible? And how are we to view human nature? The first, considered in this chapter, will help us to be faithful in our understanding and application of God's word as we counsel; the second, looked at in the next chapter, will influence how we see those whom we care for. Hopefully, too, this enquiry will enable us to evaluate the vast range of methodologies, both Christian and secular, which offer their wares in the counselling market-place. For example, it will help us appraise, from biblical perspectives, humanistic psychology, the use of hypnosis, therapies allied to the New Age Movement, trans- actional analysis, nouthetic counselling, inner healing, the use of Jungian insights by many Christians, and the deliverance ministry.[1] Even so we will always need to weigh things up with humility, for God sometimes has a knack of surprising us by using an approach which we, perhaps too hastily, have just deemed to be 'unbiblical'.

We might first ask: how do we evaluate any piece of writing? We are, I believe, forced to ask questions of the Bible as we would of any other literature. What sort of writing is it? What are its intent and content? Who wrote its constituent parts? What, or who, inspired them? Are they trustworthy and do they ring true?

In the same way, we need to address three main issues in order to clarify a biblical basis for counselling. We must consider the Bible's *content, reliability* and *interpretation*. I put the order this way round, because it is only as we examine the text that we can see what it says of itself, and thus assess its trustworthiness and know how to interpret it.

Content

It would be an interesting exercise to divide the Bible into its numerous books and ask a librarian to catalogue these into appropriate sections. This would not be a completely straightforward task but we might find, for example, that Joshua, 1 and 2 Kings, the Synoptic Gospels and Acts are placed under 'history'; that Genesis is with books on 'archaeology and anthropology'; Leviticus and Deuteronomy are under 'law'; Ruth and Job under 'biography'; the Psalms and Song of Songs under 'poetry'; Proverbs and Ecclesiastes under 'philosophy'; Isaiah, Amos and James are with 'politics and sociology'; the Pauline Epistles under 'collected letters'; and Daniel, Revelation and, perhaps, John's Gospel are under a mystical subsection of 'religious studies'.

Seeing the wide range of literary *genre* within the Scriptures enhances rather than diminishes their impact. For, as we study the Bible, whether in the account of the Israelites' wanderings in the Book of Exodus, in the imagery of the Psalter, in the warnings of Jeremiah, in the visions of Ezekiel, in the recollections of the life of Jesus by Mark or Luke, or in the hard reasoning of a letter from Paul or Peter, we find the same rich vein that can be quarried for our good. As Romans 15:4 declares of the Old Testament:

For everything that was written in the past was written to teach us, so that through endurance and the encouragement of the Scriptures we might have hope.

That hope, as the next two verses make plain, is in 'the God and Father of our Lord Jesus Christ'. From Genesis to Revelation, whatever the literary form and whoever has been involved in the writing of the original text, it is soon clear that God himself is the central subject: the Bible is *God's* story. And that story traces the dealings of the Creator with wayward humanity and the calling out of his own people, and it reaches a climax in the

sending of the Lord Jesus Christ, 'when the time had fully come
. . . to redeem those under law, that we might receive the full
rights of sons' (Gal. 4:4–5). God's 'salvation story' runs on in
the pages of the New Testament to embrace the life, death
and rising again of his Son, the sending of the Spirit and the
activity and teaching of the early Church, as the 'end-time'
begins to unfold.

As we turn to the Bible for instruction in our caring and
counselling, it is important that we remember that the Scriptures
are a God-given account of his strategy for the life and destiny
of humankind. Within the text we find narrative, highlighted
history, straight teaching, command, promise, reflection, prophecy, warning, social concern, allegory, vision, poetry, parable,
all shot through with divine and human interplay. And yet,
the Bible is a guidebook rather than a textbook: it lays down
principles and direction rather than hard-edged theory and
rigidly prescribed practice. Although the Scriptures say much
about the God who made the mountains and valleys, they do
not provide a standard text on geography and geology; although
we find recorded a great deal about monarchs, armies, battles
and treaties, the Bible is not an archive of definitive history;
although we read of the Lord of the heavenly bodies, the
Bible is not a reference book on astronomy or astrophysics.
Further, and most importantly from our point of view, although
the Bible gives us a fine treasury of insight and understanding
into human nature, it is not *primarily* a textbook on psychology
and counselling. It does not contain every piece of information
we require for understanding and reaching out to the needy,
and yet it does give us the ground rules necessary to evaluate
the theory and practice of caring. Richard Lovelace has made
the point well:

> We must guard against the assumption that all the truth that
> is needed for the most effective counselling is contained in
> Scripture. Biblical truth is not a compendium of all necessary
> knowledge, but a touchstone for testing and verifying other

kinds of truth and a structure for integrating them. It is not an encyclopedia, but a tool for making encyclopedias.[2]

Reliability

But can we trust this 'tool for making encyclopedias'? Can we depend on its content and teaching for our own lives, and for the lives of those we seek to help? Or do we feel puzzled by its welter of stories, literary form and comment?

Once more, we need to see what the Bible claims for itself, and it is here that we can turn to the statement in 2 Timothy 3:16, the yardstick of many counselling methodologies which claim to be biblical:

All Scripture is God-breathed and is useful for teaching, rebuking, correcting and training in righteousness.

A similar emphasis is given in 2 Peter 1:21 where the writer, referring to the Old Testament, declares that the prophets 'spoke from God as they were carried along by the Holy Spirit'.

It is clear from statements like these that the early Christians, using the Greek translation of the Old Testament, the Septuagint, believed that *all* of the text was, in some sense or other, moulded by God's Spirit. The word used in 2 Timothy 3:16, *theopneustos* (God-breathed), does not imply any particular theory of *how* God inspired both the oral and written traditions underlying Scripture. There is no indication, for example, of a form of divine dictation ('Paul, please take down this letter to the church of Ephesus and make sure you get the spelling and punctuation right!'), or that God in any way has bypassed the personality, experience and literary style of the various writers.

Just as the authority of the Old Testament rests on the views held by both Jesus and his followers,[3] so the God-givenness of the New Testament is implied within those very writings. For example, Jesus anticipated the work of the Holy Spirit in teaching the disciples and reminding them 'of everything I have said to you' (Jn. 14:26); Paul, in his letters, emphasised his credibility not only as God's servant but also as his apostle, a designation comparable to that of the Old Testament prophet.[4] Similar authentication was claimed by James, Peter and John at the outset of their Epistles.

Most conservative Christians would go along with the discussion so far concerning the overall reliability of the Scriptures as 'God-breathed'. However, from the late nineteenth century onwards there have been a number of attempts, in the face of the challenge of liberalism, to tighten up the way the Bible is seen – not only with respect to its inspiration, but also to its infallibility and inerrancy. One contemporary example of this perspective is seen in the Statement of Faith of the Association of Biblical Counsellors, which declares, 'I hereby affirm . . . that the Bible is the inspired, inerrant and authoritative word of God and the only authoritative standard for Christian counselling'.[5]

The niceties of language used in trying to peg out definitions of how we are to understand Holy Writ's reliability are fraught with difficulty. James Packer, who has made this debate a speciality, has written:

> Infallibility signifies the full trustworthiness of a guide that is not deceived and does not deceive.

and

> Inerrancy signifies the total truthfulness of a source of information that contains no mistakes.[6]

Although many who pin their lives on the reliability of Scripture will have no difficulty with the first statement, it is the phrase 'no mistakes' in the inerrantist's position which is open to a fuller discussion.[7] I shall highlight one or two points here.

We need to understand, first, that *none* of the original scriptural texts have survived and that the Bibles we use are translations of copies perhaps many times removed from the earliest manuscripts. Secondly, there are undeniable discrepancies in the writings as we now have them. Apart from errors which relate to the widely-held views of the day (e.g., that the sun goes round the earth) there are instances of historical inaccuracy. A simple example is found in the differences between Matthew's and Mark's account of the healing of Jairus' daughter: in Matthew 9:18ff. we read that the child had 'just died' when her father came to Jesus, whereas Mark 5:23 reveals that she was in the process of dying at that time.

Such discrepancies are not profound, but it is far from helpful, or honest, to deny their existence in the texts as we have them. Some Christians hold to a resolute view of the Scriptures which enables them never to have a problem with what they read. Professor Howard Marshall cites the example of a friend who was asked, 'Do you really believe that the whale swallowed Jonah?' and answered, 'I'd believe what the Bible says, even if it said that Jonah swallowed the whale!'[8]

Nonetheless, the line between those who hold to biblical inerrancy and those who find that term too prone to endless qualification, yet at the same time see the Scriptures as wholly trustworthy, is a narrow one. Either way, the question of the Bible's inspiration and infallibility needs to be met by a well-informed faith, based on Scripture's view of itself, coupled with the perspectives held by Jesus and the early Christians. God is able to mediate the Bible's essential reliability to us today, in spite of the presence of certain textual errors. Howard Marshall puts his finger on a right viewpoint, I believe, when he writes of these two emphases:

There may be differences between the two schools on matters of detail which are in danger of being elevated into matters of principle, but these are as nothing compared with that which they have in common, namely the belief in the entire trustworthiness of Scripture for its God-given purpose. And there is a world of difference between this position and that which would deny that the Scriptures are the inspired Word of God.[9]

Interpretation

We have seen something of the content and reliability of the Bible, and now we can ask how we are to understand and apply it. I want to explore two main areas here: the notion of a God who reveals himself; and the process of understanding and unpacking the text for our use today, as carers and counsellors.

Revelation

In searching the Scriptures, biblical theologians have established two main ways in which God reveals himself to humankind: *general revelation*, in which we discern God's power and provision in the created order, in his sovereignty over history, and in the stamp of his nature in humanity's moral sense and conscience;[10] and *special revelation*, in which we see a fuller and more specific revelation of God's nature and plans through the law and the prophets, through the oral and written traditions of Scripture, and, supremely, in the sending of his Son, 'who came from the Father, full of grace and truth' (John 1:14), and of the Holy Spirit, who has revealed 'the mystery of Christ' to 'God's holy apostles and prophets' (Eph. 3:4–5).

These two aspects of revelation complement each other. In Psalm 19, for example, verses one to six, beginning with the phrase, 'The heavens declare the glory of God', point to general revelation, whereas verses seven to fourteen, starting with 'The law of the Lord is perfect, reviving the soul', display special revelation. More profoundly, we find that Christ himself is the integration point (see Figure 1) between these two dimensions of God's disclosure: for he is both Lord of creation and Lord of the Church, the Maker and Reconciler of all things:

He is the image of the invisible God, the firstborn over all creation. For by him all things were created . . . all things were created by him and for him. He is before all things, and in him all things hold together. And he is the head of the body, the church . . . For God was pleased to have all his fulness dwell in him, and through him to reconcile to himself all things . . . by making peace through his blood, shed on the cross.(Col. 1:15–20)

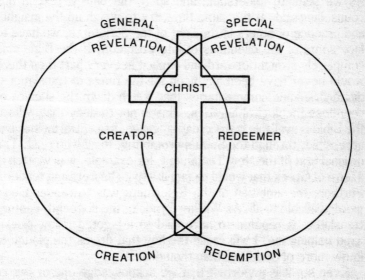

Figure 1. General and special revelation.

In our understanding and application of the Scriptures to caring and counselling, we need to keep these twin perspectives in mind. The God whom we see in the created order has also given us a mandate to be stewards over what he has made, and therein lies our call to explore, comprehend, celebrate, harness and respect the resources around us. These endeavours have been systematised through history within what we now call the arts, sciences and humanities – and these disciplines include our enquiry into counselling and psychology. At the same time, we should hold up any theory or practice of counselling to the plumb-line of Scripture. As Calvin put it, we need to look at the world around us through the 'spectacles' of God's word.[11]

Understanding the Text

1. The Dilemmas

As we seek to understand and apply the biblical text in our counselling and, at the same time, try to weigh up the insights and practice of others in the light of the Scriptures, we have to face some of the dilemmas of interpretation. If the Bible was completely straightforward and explicit in every part then there would never have been any need for the range of translations, dictionaries and commentaries that weigh down the shelves of countless theological libraries. This is not to deny that, where the Bible is available in everyday language, its central message is accessible, through the Spirit's prompting, to all who read. The original text of the New Testament, for example, was written in a form of Greek that would be familiar to its hearers and readers. Further, the ambition of the Reformers was to render God's word available to all. As William Tyndale, the sixteenth-century translator, is reputed to have said to a bigoted fellow-priest, 'God helping me, I will cause the boy that drives the plough to know more of Scripture than thou dost'.[12]

Even so, it is important that we acknowledge one or two of the difficulties of interpretation as we seek a biblical basis for today's pastoral care and counselling. The aim of understanding God's word has been well expressed by James D. Smart:

> All interpretation must have as its first step the hearing of the text with exactly the shade of meaning that it had when it was first spoken or written.[13]

However, the process of interpretation involves not only this 'first step' of seeing the original 'shade of meaning' as accurately as possible, but also a second step of reflecting on and applying that meaning within contemporary life. The technical term 'hermeneutics' (using the Greek verb *hermeneuo*, to interpret) has been coined to describe this process. Within the Scriptures themselves, we see something of this in Luke 24:25–27, where, on the road to Emmaus, Jesus chided the two devastated disciples for their slowness to believe 'all that the prophets (had) spoken', and then 'explained (interpreted, from *hermeneuo*) to them what was said in all the Scriptures concerning himself'. Here we find both the 'first step' of understanding the original text and the 'second step' of applying that meaning to the contemporary situation, in this case the suffering and rising again of the Christ.

In attempting to interpret the Scriptures today it is essential that we appraise the cultural contexts both of the passage studied and of modern society. Examples of the potential pitfalls in trying to bridge two cultures abound in the work of translators. Eugene A. Nida and William D. Reyburn cite instances of confusion: for example, the term 'beating the breast', found in the Bible as a mark of contrition, is taken by certain West Africans to indicate pride in personal achievement; the 'dragon' of the Book of Revelation, symbolising powerful malevolence, is understood by many Oriental people to be a bringer of good fortune; and, in reading Revelation 3:20, the Bazanaki tribe of East Africa might see Jesus as a thief, for it is only the unscrupulous who knock on doors to find out whether the house is unguarded.[14]

In a more general sense, how we read and understand the Bible will depend a great deal on our circumstances. There might, for example, be a tendency for those who are materially well-off and have fat bank balances, to prefer the edition of the Beatitudes given in Matthew 5:1–12, with its 'Blessed are the poor in spirit', to that given in Luke 6:20–26, with its starker 'Blessed are you who are poor' and '. . . woe to you who are rich'. The temptation to spiritualise the latter will be strong! In contrast, poverty-stricken communities who come to the Scriptures will find much to encourage them in the words and actions of the 'God of the poor'. However, there might be times when such readers are so distracted by deprivation that they fail to see other biblical perspectives, such as the need for forgiveness and a forgiving spirit.

2. The Two Horizons

Hans-Georg Gadamer, the German philosopher, has looked at the 'double-sidedness' of interpretation and put forward the helpful idea of 'two horizons', in which the viewpoints of the interpreter and the text are brought together. An illustration might help us here. In the summer, from the house where we live, we look out on a clump of tall sycamores and two mature ash trees, which collectively form a green and cooling backdrop to the rear garden, giving it both shade and privacy. Come the winter, though, the view opens up dramatically, as we gaze out through the bare branches and across the valley to a sweeping panorama of low limestone hills and the rooftops of Bristol ten miles away. Here we have two horizons: the narrow and intimate one of summer, and the wide, far-reaching one of winter. In reality, our seasonal options are not as simple as that. For in summer, with a little effort, we can climb higher up the slope near the house and then see over the trees of our garden to the wider horizon: by changing our viewpoint we have a new perspective. Conversely, in winter our narrower horizon sometimes closes in on us once more, when the valley is lost in driving rain or filled with fog.

Carrying this comparison back to Gadamer's notion, we are reminded, in our attempts to interpret the Bible, that we operate within 'two horizons'. The first is the more limited perspective brought from personal experience and from the assumptions of contemporary culture. The second is the wider vista offered by Scripture, often hidden by prejudice, pride or a lack of knowledge. We can, however, through diligent study and the Holy Spirit's leading, 'climb higher' so that our vision of God's word is enlarged as we see beyond our false presuppositions.

As Anthony Thiselton has put it:

> Even if the problems of hermeneutics are not trivial, neither
> are they insoluble, and there is always progress towards a
> fusion of horizons. The Bible can and does speak today, in
> such a way as to correct, reshape, and enlarge the interpret-
> er's own horizon.[15]

Progress towards the fusion of the two horizons within
pastoral care, though, poses questions as difficult as in any
other area of Christian concern. What, for example, do the
callings of the levitical priest and the 'wise ones' of the Wisdom
literature have to say, if anything, for today's counselling in
Christian circles? What do the miracles of Jesus declare for the
healing ministries of the contemporary Church? Is there any
relevance for spiritual direction in the discipling relationships
between Elijah and Elisha, and Paul and Timothy? How are we
to understand our notions of psychological maturity in the face of
Pauline teaching on growth into Christlikeness? What light does
the Bible shed on how we should handle the Scriptures in our
day-to-day care and counsel?

It is as we wrestle with questions like these and, in Thiselton's
words, allow Scripture to 'correct, reshape, and enlarge' our
ways of seeing that we shall be the more effective in our
caring and counselling. It was only as I had allowed the Psalms
of Lament to challenge my own understanding and mould my
response to God that I could gently point Kate, with whose story
we began this chapter, towards the realisation she needed.

Questions for Discussion

1. How do you understand the idea of the Bible's inspiration?
Is it any different to an 'inspired' piece of literature? If so, in
what way?
2. The Scriptures have been variously described as infallible,

inerrant, trustworthy and wholly true. Which terms do you find most helpful, and why?

3. Although we have not yet examined this issue in depth, it may be helpful at this stage to share in the group how you see the use of the Bible in relation to Christian caring and counselling.

4. Discuss the idea of the 'two horizons' in understanding and applying the Bible. Read Luke 10:25–37, the story of the Good Samaritan. What does this account suggest for 'crossing the barriers' of culture and race in Christian caring today?

Personal Reflection

Try to find some uninterrupted time of fifteen minutes or more. We have seen that God reveals himself in two main ways, 'general' and 'special'. First, read Psalm 19:1–6. Ask yourself how God speaks to you through the world around you. Write down your ideas.

If you can, take a walk locally and look for God in the people you meet or in solitude, in built-up areas or in the countryside, in the noise or the silence. If you are confined for any reason, look around you or out of the window. Use any senses you can: sight, hearing, smell, touch and taste.

Now, read Psalm 19:7–11 slowly and prayerfully, a couple of times. How does your view of what you read in the Bible compare to the psalmist's?

Reflect on verses 12–14 and use them as a prayer.

2
Human Nature: the Bible's View

If within us we find nothing over us, we succumb to what is around us.

P. T. Forsyth

Those of us involved in pastoral care and counselling may be forgiven if, at times, we feel that *the* problem with our work is the human factor. Life would be so much easier, or so we might think on an 'off' day, if our needy neighbours, fellow Church members or clients would keep their distance. At such times, we reckon the squabbles, tight spots, distorted ways of thinking and behaving, bad decisions and rebel emotions that others become enmeshed in are too much for us. We might even be tempted to conclude that, where human nature is at its most provoking, 'People who want by the yard but try by the inch should be kicked by the foot'.[1] And yet, of course, the dilemma lies within the counsellor as well as the client, in the carer as well as the cared for. We all suffer from a surfeit of human nature!

The reality is that how we see human nature will profoundly affect our approach to counselling. Methods influenced by behaviourism, for example, tend to view human beings as the sum-total of their patterns of behaviour; analytical theory emphasises the primacy of instinct and can lead to a pessimistic

stance where there is little hope of change; humanistic and existential ideas concentrate, more optimistically, on personhood
and the ability of the individual to develop and mature; and the
transpersonalism of the New Age Movement is inclined to see
humanity in its ecological context but, at the same time, as open
to any and every supernatural force.

Let us, then, ask how we are to view ourselves and the people
we try to help. To do this, it is necessary to unravel some of the
essential aspects of what it means to be human, in the light of
the Bible, keeping in mind the principles of content, reliability
and interpretation, discussed in chapter one. We will look at
our createdness, fallenness and destiny under three headings:
image, *idol* and *identity*.

Image

In *Mister God, This is Anna*, set in the East End of London, the
six-year-old Anna says this to Fynn, her much older companion:
'The diffrense [sic] from a person and an angel is easy. Most
of an angel is in the inside and most of a person is on the
outside'.[2] It was Fynn's view that Anna was more of an angel,
for her specialness was very much 'in the inside'. However, if
we consider our humanity as the 'image of God', we find that
who we are is tied into our 'insideness' and 'outsideness', indeed
into every aspect of what it means to be a person. We first come
across mention of our image bearing at the climax of the creation
story in Genesis 1:26–28, where we read:

> Then God said, 'Let us make man in our image, in our
> likeness, and let them rule over . . . all the earth, and
> over all the creatures . . .' So God created man in his
> own image, in the image of God he created him; male and
> female he created them. God blessed them and said to them,
> 'Be fruitful and increase in number; fill the earth and subdue
> it'.

Immediately, we see that we are a special creation, made in, and for, a special relationship with God ('in the image of God'), with one another ('male and female he created them') and with the rest of the created order ('fill the earth and subdue it'). Let us examine briefly each of these facets of our humanity.

With God

On the upright piano in our lounge, in pride of place, stands a life-sized plaster model of a right-footed boot. It is a desert-boot, one of those suede, knockabout types of footwear, much loved by teenagers in the 1970s. The ribbed sole is painted a creamy white, while the cream-buff uppers have been fashioned to reveal the character and activity of the boot's original owner. Made by our son, Simon, at the age of thirteen or so, the sculpted boot speaks of the dash, verve and scuffings of his skate-boarding years. The desert-boot is an *image* of Simon, summing up and expressing a great deal of who he was and what he did at that stage in his life.

Although the precise meaning of 'image' has been endlessly debated by scholars, when we read in Genesis, chapter one, that 'God created man in his own image' we can see something of the message of Simon's desert-boot! For, as the characterful boot declares its maker-owner so, in our humanity, we have been made to declare our Creator-Lord. Thus, we, men, women and children, have been created as *representations* of God 'in his likeness'. David Clines has emphasised the call into relationship implied in this aspect of our image-bearing:

> . . . a representation resembles the original, and re-presents its original. So in Genesis 1, man is not a mere cipher, chosen at random by God . . ., but to some extent also expresses the character of God. There is thus a spiritual relationship between God and his image which runs deeper than the inbreathing of God's spirit into man's nostrils.[3]

We are, however, more than desert-boots! Our mirroring of

God is not a surface likeness, but is written deep within every aspect of our personalities. As Genesis 2:7 puts it, 'man became a living being', energised by the God-given 'breath of life'. This vitality permeates all provinces of our humanness: spiritual, mental, volitional, emotional, aesthetic, creative, social, political and economic. Although the Old Testament uses up to eighty different terms concerning human nature, often referring to parts of the body such as the heart, liver, kidneys, loins and bowels, such terms simply signify different facets of that nature. In the New Testament, Greek words like *psyche* (soul), *pneuma* (spirit) and *soma* (body) usually indicate some aspect or other of the whole person. David Stacey has summed up this essentially biblical view of our humanity in these words:

> The Hebrew did not see man as a combination of contrasted elements, but as a unity that might be seen under a number of different aspects. Behind each aspect was the whole personality.[4]

With Others

One of my jobs as part-time lecturer at a theological college is setting and marking exam questions. A few years ago, I was impressed by a reply to a question on counselling in a paper by an East African student. He pointed out that professional counsellors in his own country, influenced by Western individualism, quite readily encourage people to divorce. He went on to write:

> One good thing in (our country) is that people are not living independently, but communally, and so it is not what people want, it is what the society wants. And here shows the difference with what may happen in the West where people are taken as individuals.

This emphasis on the individual, fostered by Victorian piety, the struggle for survival through two world wars and the cut-throat competitiveness of modern society, has often been to the detriment of the Christian Church. I am not denying the importance of the personal as we sing 'When *I* survey the wondrous cross' or 'Make *me* a channel of your peace', or declare in our creeds '*I* believe . . .', but we are in danger of neglecting a crucial aspect of our image-bearing.

In the passage from Genesis 1, quoted earlier, it is easy to miss the collective in what is said. We read, 'Then God said, "Let *us* make man in *our* image, in *our* likeness"' (v.26), 'male and female he created *them*' (v.27) and 'God blessed *them* and said to *them*, "Be fruitful . . ."' (v.28). Here we see God in relationship – Father, Son and Spirit – calling the whole of humanity into relationship as an integral part of being 'the image of God'. Walter Brueggemann, in his monumental work on the early chapters of Genesis, has put it this way:

> Only in community of humankind is God reflected. God is, according to this bold affirmation, not mirrored as an individual but as a community.[5]

Throughout this book we will keep in mind that 'community' is an essential part of our mirroring of God but, for the moment, let us highlight the phrase 'male and female he created them'. Here we may need a reminder that God calls both men and women as his image bearers: it is in our *togetherness* that we most truly represent his likeness. It is important, too, to understand that this fellowship between the sexes is wider than the more exclusive relationship of marriage. The whole of humankind is called as the image of God: women, men and children, young and old, single and married.[6]

With the Created Order

The third dimension of our call into relationship is that between our humanity and the rest of the created order. It is here we recall our distinctiveness, for it is human beings – and not the

stars and sky, the sea and earth, the mammals, birds and fish –
that are made in the image of God. We saw earlier that we are
representations, but we are also *representatives* of the Creator
within a beautiful and awesome world. As the psalmist proclaims
in praise to God, 'You made (man) a little lower than the heavenly
beings and crowned him with glory and honour', and 'You made
him ruler over the works of your hands; you put everything under
his feet' (Ps. 8:5–6).

We see in this psalm, and in the first two chapters of Genesis,
something of the freedom, power and responsibility given to us.
What it means to be free and yet responsible comes through
clearly in the account of Adam in the garden in Genesis chapter
two. Here, the man is placed in a delectable environment where
well-watered trees grow – 'trees that were pleasing to the eye
and good for food' (v.9). The man was called to a life of service,
working the garden and taking care of it. He was free to enjoy
his surroundings aesthetically and functionally – free to gaze
in wonder at a tree, free to prune and mulch it, and free to
celebrate at the end of a day's work with a feast from the
forest's fruits.

And yet he was also called to responsibility. He could rejoice
in the variety and plenty of the flora and fauna around him but
that enjoyment had its constraints. The drawing of a boundary
to human freedom is summed up in the Lord God's words to
the man:

'You are free to eat from any tree in the garden; but you
must not eat from the tree of the knowledge of good and
evil, for when you eat of it you will surely die'. (Gen.
2:16–17)

A fundamental part of our bearing God's image is to relate to
the rest of the created order with both a freedom to cultivate
and appreciate and also a responsibility to care for and control,
without exceeding God-given limits. Rightly understood, this
is a mandate for celebration. At its heart, it is what has been

called 'a theology of blessing', for God sees that his creation is good and affirms it with compassion. As Brueggemann has written:

> The blessed world is indeed the world that God intended. Delighting in the creation, God will neither abandon it nor withdraw its permit of freedom.[7]

Idol

Most people in the West, if asked what they understand by the word 'idol', would describe a carved, inanimate object, representing some deity or other, before which its makers bow down in worship. A moment's reflection, though, would reveal that anyone or anything can be an 'idol', venerated for its own sake or for representing some greater reality: media stars, top sports personalities, members of the royal family, charismatic leaders, friends, houses, money, work, sex, fashion, politics, religion, science, the arts, all can be idolised and idealised. As G. K. Chesterton has said, 'When a man ceases to worship God he does not worship nothing, he worships anything'.[8] And it is this worshipping of anything, or anyone, in God's place that is at the heart of our fall from grace. What is the influence of this idolatry on our relationship with God, with others and with the rest of the created order?

With God
A somewhat wistful view of why our humanity is less than it should be is found in Mark Twain's statement that 'Man is the creature made at the end of a week's work when God was tired'. But, as we have seen, human beings were not the haphazard product of an exhausted Creator, but rather the very peak of creation, acclaimed as 'very good'. These earthlings, given freedom and responsibility within the garden,

were to prove fickle and unreliable. Drawn by a desire to satiate the senses, even in forbidden territory, and gain a level of insight that would be regretted, the woman and the man take and eat from the prohibited tree. The outcome is an unfolding story of human rebellion and folly, in which the centre of life shifts from the worship of God to the worship of self. Brueggemann, commenting on Genesis 3:1–13, writes of Adam and Eve in their fallen state:

> There is no more mention of tending and feeding. They have no energy for that. Their interest has focused completely on self, on their new freedom and the terror that comes with it . . . They had wanted knowledge rather than trust. And now they have it. They now know more than they could have wanted to know. And there is no place to run.[9]

As we have already hinted, the mainspring of this tragedy is the human desire to test God, to breach the boundary set by divine love and wisdom. In this way, humanity snubs its call to be God's representation and representative: faithful image-bearing gives place to idolatry. The poignancy of this rebuttal is summed up well by Brian Walsh and Richard Middleton in *The Transforming Vision*:

> (God) says to his human creatures, *You* image me! Not idols. Idols are simply not adequate representations of Yahweh. That task is reserved for human beings.[10]

With Others

The pernicious effects of idolatry are seen nowhere more clearly than in human relationships: between men and women, adults and children, different races, nations, creeds and political affiliations. If you or I put ourselves first, there is no end to the damage we can do to one another. Let us look briefly at just two areas in which the image-bearing of our common humanity is fragmented by idolatry: sexism and classism. We need to remember that these two broad areas are often bound up with racism, in which there is prejudice against race, culture and nation, and ageism, where it can be an offence to be either young or old.

1. Sexism

The seeds of sexism are there in the garden in the shame of the man and woman. Their disobedience *has* opened their eyes – not to a godly wisdom but to a painful awareness 'that they were naked' (Gen. 3:7). Now, what was intimate and a wonder to them has become a source of embarrassment and potential degradation. Their desire to hide the hallmarks of their sexuality from each other is only matched by their desire to hide from their Creator. The barriers erected between the sexes are symptomatic of the barrier between wilful humanity and the Lord God who still calls, 'Where are you?' (v.9).

This heightened sense of shame before God and one another is reflected in the Lord's prediction of the 'battle of the sexes', when he says to the woman, 'Your desire will be for your husband, and he will rule over you' (v.16).[11] The seed-bed of sexism *will* bear its ugly fruit. From now on the sexes will tend to polarise, women towards subordination and servility, men towards dominance and arrogance. We see here the beginnings of the male and female stereotype, each seeing the other in a distortion of reality. Where there was a God-centred harmony and mutuality, now there is a self-centred discord and contrariness. Woman as companion, partner and lover has given way to woman as sex-object, drudge or unattainable idol: man as friend is now man as roué, bully or demi-god. Sexism, as the exploitation of perceived differences, real and imaginary, between the sexes, has come home to roost.

The results of idolatry in the area of sex and gender, wor-shipping self or the sexuality of another, are plain to see in the rest of the biblical record. In particular, we find that, whether woman is portrayed as harlot, concubine or wife, she is commonly treated as a second-class citizen. There are of course honourable exceptions to this sexism, as we shall shortly see, but, fundamentally, to be female was to be at a huge disadvantage. Women were excluded from public life, so much so that they could be divorced for talking to someone on the street, and the very sight of a woman would, so it was argued, render a Jewish religious leader unclean. Life on the domestic front was no better in that a woman's marital status was essentially that of a Gentile slave: the husband was a master to be obeyed and not the equal partner of the creation story. The menial and despised position of women is summed up in the prayer of Rabbi Judah ben Elai, written in about AD 150:

> One must utter three doxologies every day: Praise God that he did not create me a heathen! Praise God that he did not create me a woman! Praise God that he did not create me an illiterate person![12]

Male dominance, and often arrogance, have set their mark on the rest of history – not least within the Christian Church. We may not now recite Rabbi Judah's threefold doxology but Christians frequently institutionalise a distortion of this God-given sexuality. As Elaine Storkey has put it:

> Men preach, women listen. Men pray, women say 'Amen'. Men form the clergy, the diaconate or the oversight, women abide by their leadership. Men study theology, women sew for the bazaar. Men make decisions, women make the tea.[13]

2. Classism

As we have seen with sexism, the exploitation of one group of people by another occurs very early in the biblical record. In the days before the Flood it is likely that humankind's 'great wickedness' (Gen. 6:5) included the oppression of others, and Noah, in his curse on the descendants of his son, Ham, declared, 'Cursed be Canaan! The lowest of slaves will he be to his brothers' (Gen. 9:25). The rest of the Old Testament is rife with accounts of one class or race, usually the wealthy and powerful, holding another, the poor and powerless, in bondage of various kinds. Jeremiah, for example, railed against the people of God, condemning the injustices of the well-to-do, in these words of the Lord:

> 'Among my people are wicked men . . . they have become rich and powerful and have grown fat and sleek. Their evil deeds have no limit; they do not plead the case of the fatherless to win it, they do not defend the rights of the poor. Should I not punish them for this?' (Jer. 5:26–29)

Jesus met the same monolith of power in the 'teachers of the law and Pharisees', religious leaders who, on the one hand, tithed aromatic herbs – 'mint, dill and cummin' – and, on the other, neglected 'justice, mercy and faithfulness' (Matt. 23:23–24). Their attention to things and neglect of human beings was as perverse, Jesus declared, as one who strains out a gnat from his drink and then proceeds blithely to swallow a camel!

This camel-swallowing blinkeredness has been a feature of the idolatry of classism through the ages. E. M. Forster expressed the attitude well in *Howard's End*: 'We are not concerned with the very poor. They are unthinkable, and only to be approached by the statistician or the poet'.[14] This brushing aside of the really needy can be the stamp of any group of people. Professor David Donnison, writing in *Third Way*, has sought to delineate the hidden poor of Western society:

> The poor are not selected at random. They tend to be the people whom the powerful . . . can afford to neglect without endangering their own political, professional or commercial prospects. They are the people whom it is not worth training; the people for whom it is not worth opening a decent shop, or a new branch of a bank or building society; the people who do not complain if their rubbish is not removed, if their schools

rot, or their vandalised telephones are not repaired. And if they do complain, who cares?[15]

With the Created Order

Until recently we had a beautiful shrub, a type of viburnum, which flowered from November onwards and filled the front garden with fragrance during the winter months. However, last autumn its leaves began to shrivel, its few, small flowers wilted and, within a month or two, it was dead. Since then several other shrubs and a small tree nearby have begun to look sickly, possibly invaded by the same virus or fungus. A familiar and much-loved corner of the garden that used to delight the senses now begins to look like an unsuccessful plant hospital!

Like the unknown organism that has attacked our viburnum, the virus of human wilfulness and disobedience has spread its toxins to the world around. What had been a scene of self-evident delight amidst the plants and animals of the garden was now one that contained the seeds of strife and adversity. The refreshing and rewarding work of Eden now gave way to back-breaking and frustrating toil:

> To Adam (the Lord God) said, '. . . Cursed is the ground because of you; through painful toil you will eat of it all the days of your life. It will produce thorns and thistles for you, and you will eat the plants of the field. By the sweat of your brow you will eat your food until you return to the ground, since from it you were taken; for dust you are and to dust you will return'. (Gen. 3:17–19)

And so, the battle is on with a created order that has become something of an adversary. And yet, as with sexism, racism and classism, idolatry can also rear its ugly head. As Walsh and Middleton have said, 'If we do not worship God, we will focus on something in creation and elevate it to the status of divinity'.[16] This malign distortion of regard for God's good creation is at its clearest and most depressing in Romans 1:22:

Although they claimed to be wise, they became fools and exchanged the glory of the immortal God for images made to look like mortal man and birds and animals and reptiles.

Identity

Perhaps the best known episode from Alan Bleasdale's BBC teledrama series *Boys from the Blackstuff* is 'Yosser's Story'. Yosser Hughes, played by Bernard Hill, is a rough diamond, given to headbanging violence, who has been deserted by his wife. Living in Liverpool in the early 1980s, he is out of work, isolated and deserted by everyone except his three small children, a girl and two boys, who follow him faithfully in all his efforts to find employment. In his desperation, he has developed the refrain 'Gissajob!' which he repeats endlessly to anyone doing something he reckons he could do. At one point, when warned by his landlord about unpaid rent, he turns to the landlord's male companion who is holding a brief-case and says, 'Gissajob! I could do that! I can hold things! Very practised at it'. For me, though, the most poignant scene came just after his children had been forcibly removed by the authorities and he had been beaten up by the police. It was at his second meeting with a Glaswegian meths drinker when, instead of his customary greeting to a stranger, 'I'm Yosser Hughes! Everyone knows me', he said, amidst the Sunday downpour, 'I'm . . . I'm . . . I'm wet'.

In Yosser Hughes, as in all of us, whatever our circumstances, we see the heartfelt human need to have a sense of who we are and where we belong. This sense of identity, to use the technical term, is made up of both an awareness of being reasonably 'together' as a person and of valuing, at least to some extent, who we see we are. Yosser, in spite of the bitterness and degradation of his life, sought to hold on to who he was against the odds. Tragically, deserted by friends and now bereft of his children, he can no longer say, 'I'm Yosser! Everyone knows me' – for our sense of who we are has to have some bearing in the world around us.

The tragedy of Yosser Hughes, and others like him, is their condition of disconnectedness, of not belonging. All pastoral care is concerned with making connections, of helping others to see how they fit into the order of things. There are many aspects to discovering this sense of connectedness, including our need for self-understanding and self-respect. These, in turn, depend a great deal on how we are viewed by others. Where we are loved and affirmed, then our sense of who we are is strengthened; where we are neglected and rejected, we can feel lost and fragmented as a person. For many, this profound need for acknowledgment comes from the accepting love of Christ himself, though this, too, is often mediated through the practical caring of God's people. When we know we are loved, we can also learn to be more at peace with our environment – with the situations in which we are placed and with the natural order that surrounds us.

Let us, then, consider how our sense of identity is discovered and enriched in our relating – with God, with others and with the rest of creation.

With God

In Geoffrey Ahern and Grace Davie's *Inner City God*, a conversation is recorded in which one person asks, 'Do you believe in a God who can change the course of events on earth?' and receives the disarming reply, 'No, just the ordinary one.'[17] Who is this God? Is he the kind of God who can and does 'change the course of events', or is he just an 'ordinary' God?

Perhaps the simplest, and profoundest, statement made by God about himself is found when, from the burning bush, he calls Moses to go and bring God's people out of Egypt. Moses, understandably diffident at the prospect of taking on the might of Pharaoh and the Egyptian army, plays for time by asking God what name he should declare to the Israelites. We read in Exodus 3:14 that God said to Moses, 'I AM WHO I AM. This is what you are to say to the Israelites: "I AM has sent me to you"'.

Here, as in Jesus' 'I am' declarations in John's Gospel, we see that God is the only one who can say 'I am who I am', the only one whose existence does not depend on anyone or anything else. In contrast, we, as his creatures, rely on him for who we are. As Dick Keyes has put it:

> God is not a means to any other end. God is the Alpha and the Omega, the beginning and the end. Our true identity is found in accepting our status as creatures of this infinite Creator God and in rooting our sense of identity in his. Our identity is an identity derived.[18]

Here, we return to our vocation as bearers of the image of God, for it is in our image-bearing that our 'derived identity' has its full expression. Further, although we have argued that our likeness to God is obscured and distorted by our fall from grace, the Bible still regards us as divine image-bearers.[19] To use Francis Schaeffer's renowned phrase, we are 'glorious ruins': like some ruined abbey, a broken arch here, an incomplete colonnade there, we are only a shadow of our original glory as bearers of God's image before the world. But, the Bible clearly states, the glory can be re-established, the image restored. And this glory, this image, is recoverable in our relationship with God through Christ. It is as we become more Christlike that God is more truly seen, for Christ is 'the image of the invisible God' (Col. 1:15).

But the process is not a quick one. The ruin is being restored, but gradually so – stone by stone, through the work of the Holy Spirit and the response of obedient lives. As Paul declares in 2 Corinthians 3:18:

> And we, who with unveiled faces all reflect the Lord's glory, are being transformed into his likeness with ever-increasing glory, which comes from the Lord, who is the Spirit.[20]

With Others

The Creator God has made us, his creatures, creative, and that creativity, part and parcel of who we are, reaches out to others. A mother gave each of her three daughters a small plot in the garden. The first tended the area with meticulous care, always remembering to water the patch and pull up the weeds: she grew up to become a caring, nurturing mother. The second, allowing the weeds to grow, became a radical who fought for the underdog. The third put up a table outside the front gate and sold lettuce, radishes and cut flowers to passers-by: she later worked as a tax inspector.[21] As each of these girls grew into womanhood she expressed her creativity and, in interaction with others, discovered her identity. As David G. Benner the psychologist has written:

> The quest for identity is sometimes incorrectly defined as an introspective retreat from others, a kind of examination of one's psychic navel. However, to attempt to find self apart from others is to fail to find our true selves. True selfhood is a gift we receive from others; in relationship to others we find who we truly are.[22]

Here, once more, we are reminded, with Brueggemann, that we mirror God best 'as a community'. And this God-mirroring community is, in spite of all its faults, the Church, the 'body' of Christ.

Pictures of the Church in the Bible include both the personal and the corporate, the individual and the collective. God's people are variously described as the 'body', with Christ as 'head' (Rom. 12:4–5; 1 Cor. 12:12–27; Eph. 4:16; Col. 1:18), as God's 'building' (1 Cor. 3:9; Eph. 2:19–22; 1 Pet. 2:5), God's 'field' (1 Cor. 3:9), a 'holy nation' (Phil. 3:20; 1 Pet. 2:9), a 'royal priesthood' (1 Pet. 2:5,9). In this imagery, although Christians are individually parts of the 'body', building stones, plants in the field, citizens and priests, the emphasis is on *connectedness* for the sake of the whole. This 'one-anotherness', or interdependence, turns its back on 'me-onlyness', which can be expressed in a proud independence or self-seeking dependency. Followers of Christ, for example, are called to 'accept one another' (Rom. 15:7), 'forgive . . . one another' (Col. 3:13), 'have . . . concern for each other' (1 Cor. 12:25), 'bear with one another' (Eph. 4:2), 'submit to one another' (Eph. 5:21), 'carry each other's burdens' (Gal. 6:2), 'admonish one another' (Col. 3:16), 'encourage each other' (1 Thes. 4:18), 'confess your sins to each other' (Jas 5:16), 'spur one another on' (Heb. 10:24), 'offer hospitality to one another' (1 Pet. 4:9) and, summarising and filling out all other injunctions, in the words of Christ's new commandment, to 'love one another' (John 13:34). It is in this call for the people of God to demonstrate 'one-anotherness' that we find the impetus of all pastoral care and, as we shall see in chapter four, its expression through counselling, the healing ministries and spiritual direction. One of the cardinal results of the mandate for Christians to love one another is found in Paul's declaration in Galatians 3:28, a statement that has been described as 'the Magna Carta of Humanity':[23]

There is neither Jew nor Greek, slave nor free, male nor female, for you are all one in Christ Jesus.

Paul is not denying the reality of distinctions between race, class, and sex and gender, but he is claiming that, in and through God's image-bearing people, the barriers erected by sexism, racism and classism should be broken down.

The demolition of such partitions is seen clearly in the life of Jesus. Just to take one instance, we can observe that, in the encounter with the woman at the well described in John 4:1–42, the Lord breaks a whole set of social taboos: those of sex, gender and class, by speaking with a woman alone; of conventional wisdom by relating to this particular woman, who had a local reputation for promiscuity; and of religion and race by making contact with a Samaritan, someone despised by any self-respecting Jew. Jesus, bearing God's likeness, stormed the barricades built by human pride and prejudice; the Church, if it is also to bear God's likeness, is to do the same.

Such enterprise is never easy, because society, and sadly often our brothers and sisters, resists change within life's comfortable structures. But the call is clear and the effort is always worthwhile, even though results may be slow in coming. One recent attempt was made in South Africa by a group of Christians, called 'Koinonia', to encourage white people to visit townships and so meet black Africans in their own surroundings. The response was modest, but of great value to the few who ventured. One white man, Alan Dawson, the mayor of Midrand near Johannesburg, admitted that for thirty-six years he had been 'indoctrinated to fear the black man' and that he half-anticipated that his fears would prove well-grounded. However, after a weekend at the township of Tembisa, he said, 'It turned out that I had gone with fear into an environment of total warmth that totally embraced me. So much so that almost immediately I felt incredibly embarrassed and foolish about my fears'.[24]

And so we see that, through the 'ministry of reconciliation' which Paul writes of in 2 Corinthians 5:16–21 and whereby we find peace with God through the death of his Son, the obstacles that divide us can be removed – whether they are between individuals, classes or races. They can all be brought together by the work of the Father, Son and Spirit. As it is said in Ephesians 2:13–14, with reference to the healing of the breach between Jew and Gentile:

But now in Christ Jesus you who once were far away have been brought near through the blood of Christ. For he himself is our peace, who has made the two one and has destroyed the barrier, the dividing wall of hostility . . .

This identity, this coming together as a coherent whole, which we have as the people of God, is very precious. It challenges

us all to continuing 'one-anotherness', as expl___
care and loving counsel spurred on by God's ___
undaunted by the irritations and frustrations of o___
Michael Walker, pastor, teacher and theologian, ___
a large vision for the Church who also faced ___ ___ ___ or
personal suffering, through the death of his first wife with
cancer and from his dying of the same condition. His lectures
on Christian spirituality at the University of Wales College of
Cardiff drew Baptist, Presbyterian and Catholic students alike.
He wrote this in his last book, *The God of Our Journey*, on
the destiny of the Church, the Bride of Christ, and her call to
faithfulness:

> Yet the Church is all that we have. It is that fair creature that,
> one day, will run in breathless adoration to meet the one who,
> from the beginning has loved her. If now, there are times
> when she is less than mindful of the maturity of her children,
> it is not for them to find maturity by forsaking her . . .[25]

With the Created Order

Hannah Hauxwell, tough and weather-beaten and a spinster in
her early sixties, looked out over a much-loved reservoir near to
her isolated, upland farm in the Yorkshire Dales. Clearly upset,
as she contemplated the imminent move to a neighbouring village for health reasons after fifty-nine years of spartan existence
at the farm, she waved her arm to indicate the scenery and said,
'Whatever I am, wherever I am, *this* is me!'[26]

As we have seen, this intimate link between a woman or
a man and the landscape is as old as humankind. We are
creatures within the created order, and that, under God, is
where we belong. Although humanity has fallen from grace,
distorting its imaging of God and making way for idolatry, the
earth, though fallen too, is still a good place to be. We catch
something of the God-centredness of this delight in Proverbs
8:22–31, where wisdom is personified (as Christ himself, some
believe) as a co-Creator:

Then (at the beginning of the Lord's work) I was the craftsman at his side. I was filled with delight day after day, rejoicing always in his presence, rejoicing in his whole world and delighting in mankind. (Prov. 8:30–31)

The Bible communicates throughout – in the early chapters of Genesis, in the Book of Job, the Psalms, Proverbs, Isaiah, the sayings and parables of Jesus, the Prologue of John's Gospel and in the great christological passages of the first chapters of Ephesians and Colossians – a high view of creation. In every place the value of the created order is affirmed by a God who loves what he has made. As Brueggemann has written:

> The creation, then, is not an object built by a carpenter. It is a vulnerable partner whose life is imparted by the voice of one who cares in tender but firm ways.[27]

This 'tender but firm' caring has led to the unfolding of a plan of restoration and renewal, focused on fallen humanity but all-inclusive of the creation itself. Paul the apostle seems to wrestle with the imponderability of this destiny in Romans 8:18–21:

> I consider that our present sufferings are not worth comparing with the glory that will be revealed in us. The creation waits in eager expectation for the sons of God to be revealed. For the creation was subjected to frustration, not by its own choice, but by the will of the one who subjected it, in hope that the creation itself will be liberated from its bondage to decay and brought into the glorious freedom of the children of God.

Paul continues his theme by pointing out that, in spite of the present reality in which both 'the whole creation' and the people of God 'groan' in anguish, there is an eager anticipation of glory to come. Whatever this difficult passage means, it strongly suggests that, through the path of sharing in Christ's sufferings, the futures of a liberated created order and of our redeemed humanity are inextricably interwoven. Further, it is important to see that the wonder of this destiny is set by Paul in Romans 8 in the wider context of the Trinity's loving action. Jürgen Moltmann has brought together this ultimate work of grace in these words:

> The creation of the world, the reconciliation, and the final redemption of the world is nothing other than the history of the changing communal relationships of the Triune God; it is the great love story of the Father, the Son, and the Holy Spirit, a divine love story in which we all are involved together with heaven and earth.[28]

An Overview

Although this has been a long chapter, it is important that we establish just how we, as carers and counsellors, are to view both ourselves and those we try to help. For it is in having a clear perspective on what the Bible says about our human nature that we are better equipped in the assumptions, aims and methods of our approaches to pastoral care and counselling.

We have seen, firstly, that we are made as God's image, men and women who are living unities, called to mirror his likeness and represent him within the created order. We have noted, too, that although we have squandered our God-given freedom and responsibility, we are still 'made in his image' even after the fall: the image is distorted in every aspect of our lives, yet not obliterated or lost. And so, our approach to counselling, as to all forms of Christian care, should be marked by a deep respect for our humanity, a discernment that, however obscured, there will be something of God's likeness even in the most damaged lives. By the same token, we should be wary of those methodologies which seem to belittle the specialness of people, reducing them to the sum-total of their instincts or appraising them merely as a network of conditioned reflexes. Moreover, we need to avoid an approach to counselling, not rare amongst Christians, which denies that God is at large in his world, and thus tends to dismiss the needy, who cannot be defined as 'born again', 'committed' or 'one of us', as outside the pale.

Secondly, we have explored the sad reality that human nature is fallen and that a great deal of human uniqueness has been spoiled by the banality and sameness engendered by sin. As Pascal said, 'Man is born an original but dies a copy'. We have seen too that the heart of this fall from grace is an idolatry which worships self and others, leading to all manner of injustice and exploitation in human relationships. We need styles of counselling which take seriously the gravity and pervasiveness of sin, and which can discern its workings in society as well as in individual lives. Approaches that are strongly influenced by the more optimistic forms of humanism, and that ignore human fallibility, emphasising the sufficiency of the self and elevating the human quest for autonomy, miss the realism of the biblical analysis.

And, finally, we have rejoiced in the glorious hope of a restored identity in Christ, personally and collectively, in and through the Church, and in close harmony with a renewed created order. Here we are reminded that we are called to 'one-anotherness' and that our individual and corporate change into Godlikeness is a gradual process, initiated and continued by the work of the Spirit. We are to beware of types of counselling that are basically pessimistic, anticipating very little effect on disordered lives and often demanding much time and money in doing so! Caution is needed, too, where certain approaches offer a 'hotline' to God and an immediate resolution of all difficulties, seemingly ignoring biblical images of step-by-step growth and the call to patient endurance. We are, rather, to take courage and offer genuine hope to needy people. Lives that are opened to the Father's compassion, the Son's friendship and the Spirit's empowering can be changed: personal freedom and responsibility can be rediscovered, and barriers between the sexes, races and classes can be broken down. With this perspective, our caring and counselling will be a 'ministry of reconciliation', reuniting people with their God, with one another and with their environment.

Questions for Discussion

1. What do you understand by the term 'made in the image of God'? Genesis 1:26–28, 2:7–25 and Psalm 8 may help you in your discussion.
2. How does an understanding that the people you care for and counsel are 'made in God's image', though the likeness is marred, affect your attitude to them?
3. Discuss the view that if God is not worshipped, then anything or anyone will be worshipped. Name some of the things that you find hard not to idealise or idolise.
4. Jesus calls us from proud independence and selfish clinging, to depend on the Father and to interdependence (see, for example, John 6:38, 8:54–56, 13:34–35, 15:12–17). Discuss how reliance on God and a sense of 'one-anotherness' should influence our caring.
5. Discuss the ways sexism, racism, classism and other prejudices can be overcome in Christian caring. Share any personal difficulties about this enterprise.

Personal Reflection

Read Proverbs 8:22–31 slowly and reflectively a couple of times. At a third reading, in imagination, hear Jesus Christ, who 'was with God in the beginning' (John 1:2), speak the words of this passage. Thank him that he rejoices in the created world, and delights in you.

Take a piece of paper and complete twenty 'I am . . .' statements. Do not worry if you find it difficult to say things about yourself after the first more obvious statements: 'I am a human being', 'I am a woman', 'I am a father', 'I am a sister', etc. Ask God to help you to be honest and show you your strengths and weaknesses. Thank him that who you are is linked with who he is. These words by John Newton may help at the end of this exercise:

> I am not what I ought to be; I am not what I would like to be; I am not what I hope to be. But I am not what I once was; and by the Grace of God, I am what I am.

Read Matthew 6:19–21 and think over Jesus' words: 'For where your treasure is, there your heart will be also'. Your 'treasure' is the things, ideas or people (including yourself!) you most value. Spend a few minutes thinking who or what these are. It may help to write them down. We are called to store up 'treasures in heaven', putting God first in every area of our lives. Ask him to help you find his priorities in your life. Dedicate the people, ideas and things you esteem most into his hands, seeking to obey him in all relationships and priorities. These words of the last verse of a hymn by Jenny Hewer may be used as a prayer:

> Father, I want to be with You
> And do the things You do,
> Father, I want to speak the words
> That You are speaking too.
> Father, I want to love the ones
> That You will draw to You,
> For I know that I am one with You.[29]

3

Pastoral Care: the Church's Call

All this . . . comes from the Lord Almighty, wonderful in counsel and magnificent in wisdom.

Isaiah 28:29

All compassion, justice and wisdom ultimately come 'from the Lord Almighty.' In trying to understand how Christian caring and counselling fit into today's bewildering array of remedies for humanity's ills, we need to remember this. It is God's love that motivates and empowers his people, in spite of all their inadequacies, to reach out caringly to the needy. The diminutive Anna, in Fynn's *Mister God, This is Anna*, once more has the right perspective:

> . . . Mister God is different. You see, Fynn, people can only love outside and can only kiss outside, but Mister God can love you right inside, and Mister God can kiss you right inside, so it's different. Mister God ain't like us; we are a little bit like Mister God, but not much yet.[1]

This 'different', self-giving love of God is clear throughout the pages of Scripture. We see him as Friend, who spoke to Moses 'face to face, as a man speaks with his friend' (Exod. 33:11) and, in the life and death of his Son, showed that his followers should no longer be called servants, but the sort of friends who shared the Father's secrets (John 15:13–15). Using more intimate language, the Bible shows him to be Lover, the one who commanded Hosea to love his wayward wife 'as the Lord loves the Israelites' (Hos. 3:1) and promises the consummation of his love for his people in the 'wedding of the Lamb' (Rev. 19:7). Most familiar of all, God is Father, the one who 'has compassion on his children' (Ps. 103:13) and to whom, through the Spirit's work, we cry, 'Abba, Father' (Rom. 8:15; Gal. 4:6). God is also Mother, as is shown in the begetting and nurturing imagery of Scripture, in the one who says to his people, 'As a mother comforts her child, so will I comfort you' (Isa. 66:13) and who, grieving at Jerusalem's hard-heartedness, cries, 'how often I have longed to gather your children together, as a hen gathers her chicks under her wings, but you were not willing' (Matt. 23:37). Besides pictures of God based on human relating, there are other titles which demonstrate one aspect or other of his caring work. These include that of Healer, where he declares 'I am the Lord who heals you' (Exod. 15:26) and shows this in the innumerable acts of mercy carried out by his incarnated Son, bringing restoration and wholeness to suffering people. Finally we find God – not surprisingly as the context of the Bible is largely agrarian – described as Shepherd, the one who protects and guides his flock, gathering 'the lambs in his arms', gently leading 'those that have young' (Isa. 40:11) and, supremely, laying down his life for the sheep (John 10:11–18).

In all these analogies of God's nature, the Lord is both example and, literally, inspiration to his people in their caring: literally, because it is in the inspiring, or in-breathing, of the Holy Spirit that the faithful are given the power and motivation to follow the divine example. And so, the people of God are called and empowered to befriend, love, be fatherly and motherly, to heal and to shepherd others. Here is the mandate for the 'one-anotherness' that we discussed in the last chapter, a mutual caring that is primed by the love of

God. As John puts it, 'We love because he first loved us' (1 John 4:19).

This calling is perhaps best summed up in the words of Leviticus 19:18, 'love your neighbour as yourself', a command that is frequently repeated in the Bible but always in the wider context of loving God.[2] The Greek *ho plesion*, the neighbour, indicates whoever is nearby and, as Jesus' story of the Good Samaritan shows, neighbourly love knows no bounds – both in the giving and receiving. Commenting on the parable of Luke 10:25–37, and the way God's love moves through our humble acts of loving to bring forth love in the recipient, Ulrich Falkenroth has written:

> Christ meets me in the other person, whether he is brother or enemy, neighbour or godless, helper or beggar. He gives me his love and fills me with it, so that it flows over to the other. This moves love to my neighbour out of the dangerous region of new legalism, or proud charity, and puts it under the sway of love, which both takes and gives.[3]

What is Pastoral Care?

There have been many attempts throughout Church history to define the expression of Christian love. One tradition, looking to the Latin word *cura*, which can mean either cure or care, has put forward the twin elements of 'soul cure', seeking remedy for sin, and 'soul care', emphasising growth in spiritual maturity. However, the distinction between these two activities is far from clear and the terms are now generally obsolete. More helpfully, Jacob Firet, drawing on the use of three Greek words, subdivides Christian ministering into: the *Kerygma* (preaching), in which God's offer of new life in Christ is proclaimed;[4] the *Didache* (teaching), whereby the people of God are instructed in the way of discipleship;[5] and the *Paraklesis* (exhorting, consoling), which centres on the 'one-anotherness' of the Church.[6] Although there is clearly overlap between preaching, teaching and the ministry of exhortation and consolation, it is in this third area that we come to the heart of Christian caring. Firet sums up this 'paracletic' work with these words:

> . . . paraklesis is the mode in which God comes to people in their situations of dread, suffering, sin, despair, error, and insufficiency. God comes to persons to rescue them out of the distress of their situation in order to bring them into life with the church in the enjoyment of the salvation which is in Christ, comforted and courageous in the joy of new obedience. God leads them through this process to their own places and makes them fit to fulfil special tasks within the body of Christ.[7]

This paracletic ministry (including, amongst other perspectives, all the nuances of *parakaleo*, to ask, invite, exhort, encourage, comfort and console) is the essence of 'pastoral care'. This latter term is a generally accepted one for the Church's overall caring and, like most 'umbrella' words, is difficult to pin down. In a different context, Thomas à Kempis wrote, 'I would far rather feel contrition than be able to define it',[8] and we may respond similarly in trying to define pastoral care. We would far rather feel forgiveness, receive encouragement or experience practical help than attempt to describe the process behind these acts of mercy. Nonetheless, for the sake of our understanding of Christian caring and counselling we do need a working definition. One that has held stage since the late 1960s is that of Clebsch and Jaekle in their *Pastoral Care in Historical Perspective*, in which they declare:

> The ministry of the cure of souls, or pastoral care, consists of helping acts, done by representative Christian persons, directed towards the healing, sustaining, guiding, and

reconciling of troubled persons whose troubles arise in the context of ultimate meanings and concerns.[9]

Although this explanation of pastoral care is still a useful one it can be criticised on a number of grounds.[10] Amongst these are its commitment to individuals of the ordained ministry (understandable in a North American context) as the sole 'representative Christian persons' involved in pastoral care, and its neglect of the corporate and communal. Keeping in mind our call to 'one-anotherness' and 'good-neighbourliness', I would like to define pastoral care as *the practical expression of the Church's concern for the everyday and ultimate needs of both its members and the community*. This definition allows for the comprehensiveness of pastoral care – dealing with 'everyday' issues such as illness, decision making and forgiving others, as well as 'ultimate' needs such as peace with God and maturity in Christ. It also covers the reality that pastoral care is the province of both ordained pastors and responsible lay people, and indicates the importance of the collective aspects, such as overall Church strategy, the resolving of group conflicts, and communal issues on, amongst others, housing, unemployment and conservation.

The Story of Pastoral Care

The 'one-anotherness' and 'good-neighbourliness' of pastoral care, including Clebsch and Jaekle's strands of healing, sustaining, reconciling and guiding, have been the hallmarks of the Church at its truest down the ages. Many of us are unaware of this rich heritage, within which countless men and women, their work and devotion often unsung, have prayed, laboured and loved in the name of Christ.[11] Amongst the many whose Christian caring has been recorded, we can single out only a representative few.

In the earlier centuries, the letters of Cyprian (c.200–258),

Bishop of Carthage, written to encourage the faithful during persecution, the medical caring and hospital founding of Basil the Great (329–379) and the wide influence of the *Pastoral Rule* by Gregory the Great (540–604) may be mentioned. During the superstitious days of the Middle Ages, the practical spirituality of Bernard of Clairvaux (1090–1153) and the profound commitment to the poor and despised by Francis of Assisi (1181–1226) were outstanding. In the following centuries, the lives and writings of a number of Christian mystics, including Julian of Norwich (c.1342–1420), Catherine of Siena (c.1347–1380), Teresa of Avila (1515–1583) and John of the Cross (1542–1591), brought renewed insight into God's faithful love, and underlined the need for self-knowledge, in and through life's adversities.

The Reformation, with its return to biblically-based faith and action, rediscovered some of the key strands of pastoral care, including the element of reconciliation, as seen in the *Fourteen Consolations* by Martin Luther (1483–1546) and in the Church discipline emphasised by John Calvin (1509–1564). It was towards the end of the next century, particularly through Richard Baxter (1615–1691) and his *Reformed Pastor*, that pastoral care began to be systematised into pastoral theology.

During the Evangelical Revival, John Wesley (1703–1791), influenced by Count Ludwig von Zinzendorf (1700–1760) and the Moravians, introduced small groups of Christians committed to mutual nurture, devotion to God and social action. Here was a fully-rounded pastoral care which involved women and men alike as lay ministers and, as well as including the strands of reconciliation, sustainment and guidance, offered healing through the foundation of free health clinics and through the influence of Wesley's best-selling *Primitive Physick* (1747).

The nineteenth century, in the face of the Industrial Revolution, besides stressing individual piety, saw a pastoral care which reached out impressively to the disadvantaged both directly and through social reform. The compassion and campaigning of William Wilberforce (1759–1833) and the Clapham Sect, amongst Evangelicals, and the practical acts of mercy carried out by newly-founded religious communities in the Catholic tradition, are prime examples of this love in action.

The Rise of Counselling

Ever since Adam and Eve sought solace in each other's arms, there have been attempts to meet the needs of others and of the self. As we noted in the last chapter, these attempts are inevitably influenced by the view of humanity held by the participants. Pastoral care through the ages has been no exception to this rule. Even though the Church has often aimed to be true to biblical perspectives on human nature, it is also unavoidable that it has been influenced to some extent by the prevailing mind-set of its environment. At best, the people of God have sifted, evaluated and challenged contemporary thinking in the light of Scripture; at worst, they have found the approach of the 'two horizons' (see pp. 14–15) too daunting and have either escaped into the bolt-hole of reaction or embraced the cosy anonymity of assimilation, taking in the presuppositions and objectives of the surrounding culture with little or no critical reflection. It is with the rise of secular psychologies during the nineteenth and twentieth centuries that pastoral care has been most pressed to respond to such contrary influences.

Rise of the Secular Psychologies

By the beginning of the nineteenth century, ways of viewing humanity were dividing into two main strands: mental philosophy, which concentrated on the so-called 'mental faculties' of reason, will, memory and emotions; and the empirical sciences, which focused on what was observable and measurable. A whole range of psychological understandings came into being, seeking to emphasise either the 'inner' or 'outer' life of those they studied, while, increasingly from the mid-twentieth century onwards, efforts were also made to synthesise the two. Amidst this welter of theorising four main streams can be discerned: behaviourism, psychoanalysis, personalism and transpersonalism.[12]

The following diagram, showing the four main sectors of counselling and psychotherapy, may be helpful at this stage:[13]

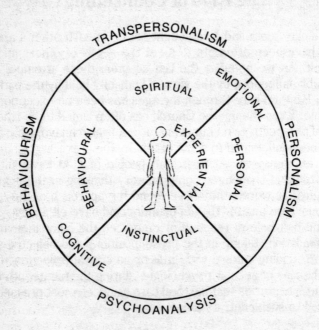

Figure 2. Secular approaches to counselling and therapy.

Behaviourism, par excellence, sought to define humanity simply in terms of what can be seen and recorded. Its founding father can be said to be the Soviet physiologist, Ivan Pavlov (1849–1936) who based his theories of human nature on the beliefs that the universe is one, impersonal reality, that all behaviour is rigidly tied to its cause and that human beings are merely higher animals. Here is a reductionist view that debases the biblical concept of human beings as the image of God. In fairness though to Pavlov, and to other influential behaviourists like John B. Watson (1878–1958), B. F. Skinner (1904–), Joseph Wolpe (1915–) and Hans J. Eysenck (1916–), behaviourism has generated a great deal of invaluable research into human behaviour and has, in turn, given rise to many useful techniques in counselling.[14] On the dehumanising philosophy of unadulterated behaviourism, W. H. Auden has written:

> Of course, 'Behaviourism' works. So does torture. Give me a no-nonsense, down-to-earth behaviourist, a few drugs, and simple electrical appliances, and in six months I will have him reciting the Athanasian creed in public.[15]

In the second half of the twentieth century, however, there have emerged a number of schools of therapy which have tackled behavioural problems through people's ways of thinking. These less reductionist approaches include Albert Ellis' rational-emotive therapy,[16] William Glasser's reality therapy and, most recently, the cognitive-behavioural counselling of Aaron Beck and others.

Psychoanalysis, in contrast to behaviourism, examines the inner life, assuming that the individual is the sum of his or her instincts. Sigmund Freud (1856–1939), the pioneer of psychoanalysis, offered an 'archaeology of the mind', delving into the hidden past, in his so-called 'talking cure'. He argued that personality is based on biological drives that are mainly sexual in nature and that it develops through a series of inevitable stages during the first five years of life. Freudianism, as with all innovative movements, has its purists, modifiers and dissentients:[17] Anna Freud (1895–1982), Sigmund's daughter, amplified his views, stressing the importance of the ego, – the conscious, evaluating aspect of a person, and 'defence mechanisms', those 'psychological suits of armour' worn by all of us at some stage or other; Melanie Klein (1882–1960), with her followers, stressed the vital nature of the first year of life; Carl Jung (1875–1961) broke from Freud over the latter's undue stress on sexuality – his analytical psychology, with its awareness of the supernatural and the 'shadow' side of life, has influenced many Christians;[18] finally, 'Neo-Freudians', like Karen Horney (1885–1952) and Erich Fromm (1900–1980), have emphasised the social dimension. As is indicated, psychoanalysis embraces a wide range of ideas, from the pessimism of Freud, seeing people as bound by their inner drives, to the more socially aware and hopeful views of later thinking.

Personalism, which includes both humanistic and existential approaches, carries the optimism of the neo-Freudians further. Born in the thinking of German philosophers and psychologists at the end of the nineteenth century, it has been given its greatest publicity in the work of Carl Rogers (1902–1987), who has argued that people have within themselves all the resources needed for growth in maturity. As we shall see, Rogers' humanism, his non-directive style and emphasis on the client were of great significance in the rise of counselling during the 1940s and 1950s. Whereas behaviourism and psychoanalysis tend to reduce our humanity, this 'third force' of humanistic psychology is inclined to inflate it. At its best, it is in touch with the value and reality of what it is to be human; at its worst, it can lead to 'selfism', an idolatry which believes that the individual's thoughts and feelings are more important than anything else.[19]

Transpersonalism, arising from the seed-bed of Western humanism and Eastern mysticism, seeks fulfilment beyond the personal in the realms of the Higher Self, Unity Consciousness, the Cosmos or God. It seems that many humanistic and existential thinkers, having denied or ignored God, have seen the bankruptcy of their theories and have sought significance outside themselves. It was Abraham Maslow (1903–1970) who moved from traditional humanism to this 'Fourth Force' psychology and wrote:

Without the transcendent and transpersonal, we get sick, violent, and nihilistic, or else hopeless and apathetic. We need

something 'bigger than we are' to be awed by and to commit
ourselves to in a new, naturalistic, empirical, non-churchly
sense . . .[20]

Other exponents of transpersonalist psychology include George
Gurdjieff (c.1875–1949), Peter Ouspensky (1878–1947) and
Oscar Ichazo (1931–), variously influenced by Yoga, Sufism,
Buddhism and Christian monasticism; and Roberto Assagioli
(1888–1974), whose 'psychosynthesis', using music therapy
and imaginative journeying, aims at a sense of harmony within
the person, in relationships and with the universe. It is the
theorising of approaches like these, seeking integration within
the natural order – an integration that can only be met fully in
Christ, that has been so influential on the so-called New Age
Movement. This movement is a ragbag of loosely connected
emphases, ranging from the murky waters of occultism to a
genuine care for the environment and concern for the oppressed. Here there is a pressing need for a Christian critique,
affirming, on the one hand, that the 'earth is the Lord's' and
all responsible stewardship should be welcomed, and, on the
other hand, resisting all that worships the created rather than
the Creator.

Crisis in Pastoral Care

There is no doubt that the age-old tradition of pastoral care
has been threatened by the rise of atheistic and agnostic
psychologies during the nineteenth and twentieth centuries.
God had spoken 'in times past' and now many other, often
alien, voices could be heard offering alternative remedies for
the needs of humanity. Thomas C. Oden, in his seminal
paper 'Recovering Lost Identity', has pointed to a failure of
nerve amongst Christian carers, suggested by a comparison
of standard works on pastoral theology, written at the turn
of the century, with those on pastoral counselling, produced

in the 1950s and 1960s.[21] In the former he observed a generous sprinkling of references to such figures as Cyprian, Augustine, Luther and Baxter, whereas the indexes of the latter were devoid of the major Christian pastors of history, being filled rather with the names of Freud, Jung, Rogers and Fromm. What were the reasons for this marked change of emphasis?

Perhaps, at its profoundest, the underlying cause relates most to the fact that pastoral care was as vulnerable to the world-views of the Enlightenment, or Age of Reason, as any aspect of society. Since the middle of the eighteenth century, a form of scientific enquiry which excluded the supernatural and which elevated rationality increasingly held centre-stage. Lesslie Newbigin has captured the essence of this all-embracing development well:

> To have discovered the cause of something is to have explained it. There is no need to invoke purpose or design as an explanation. There is no place for miracles or divine intervention in providence as categories of explanation. God may be conceived . . . as the ultimate author of it all, but one does not need to know the author personally in order to read the book. Nature – the sum total of what exists – is the really real. And the scientist is the priest who can unlock for us the secrets of nature and give us the practical mastery of its workings.[22]

This elevation of the scientist, including the psychologist, to priest, and of nature to the 'really real' began to infiltrate the caring ministry of the Church towards the end of the nineteenth century, gaining powerful momentum from the 1920s onwards. Tragically, God's people were especially susceptible to the advances of the secular psychologies due to an inadequate theology of creation and a poor concept of common grace. Instead of rejoicing in scientific discovery and celebrating the Creator, Christians were often either wrong-footed into rejecting the results of research, along with the atheistic views of the researchers, or they swallowed the new perspectives hook, line and sinker. In time, fortunately, there has emerged a third group, which is prepared for dialogue between theology and psychology, between pastoral care and secular counselling.[23]

Caring and Counselling Today

The legacy of the interplay between traditional pastoral care and the emerging secular psychologies in the first half of the twentieth century has left three broad positions amongst Christians: assimilative, reactive and a readiness for dialogue. Increasingly, individuals, churches and other caring Christian organisations can be shown to have a mixture of stances, where some aspects of secular psychology are assimilated, others are rejected and yet others are seen as worthy of dialogue.

The *assimilative* position has its roots in the alliance between the Church and the new psychological understandings. Washington Gladden, a Congregational minister from Ohio, for example, urged in the 1890s a closer tie between the clergy and the medical profession, while, in 1905 a group of Episcopalians in Boston, Massachusetts, formed the Emmanuel Movement which declared that the care of souls should now be guided by 'the science of psychotherapy'. It was Anton T. Boisen (1876–1966), the pioneer of training ordinands in the setting of psychiatric hospitals, who warned the emerging Clinical Pastoral Education (CPE) of the danger of an uncritical acceptance of Freudianism. Broadly speaking, the so-called 'pastoral counselling movement', spearheaded by CPE and enhanced by the work of the Westminster Pastoral Foundation in the United Kingdom, has assimilated a great deal of analytic and personalist thinking and practice, although it offers much of value in its comprehensive training programmes.

Inevitably, *reactive* views grew in the face of the apparent love affair between liberal Christianity and Freud and friends. These more conservative stances range from a general dismissal of all secular psychology to positions that point out the subversive aspects of alien views. Examples within this spread include Eduard Thurneysen (1888–1974), influenced by Karl Barth and stressing the centrality of the word of God in pastoral care, and, in more recent years, O. Hobart Mowrer, the behaviourist, and Jay Adams, initially indebted to Mowrer and the pioneer of 'nouthetic' (based on the Greek *noutheteo*, to admonish, to exhort) counselling. Whereas assimilative views tend to focus on God's general revelation to the neglect of special revelation (see pp. 10–12), reactive positions often reverse this trend.

Fortunately, the more polarised viewpoints just outlined have been increasingly questioned and debated by those engaging in *dialogue*. Here, in effect, a God who speaks both generally through his creation and specifically through Christ is acknowledged. Proponents of this broad position include Christians of conservative, liberal and radical persuasions, who seek a measure of integration between theological and psychological insight. Important voices in this continuing debate include Frank Lake (1914–1982), Robert Lambourne (1917–1972), Alastair V. Campbell and Stephen Pattison in the United Kingdom, and Thomas Oden, Don S. Browning, Donald Capps, Mary Stewart Van Leeuwen and David G. Benner in the United States.

As we survey the scene of Christian caring today we can see, amidst the ferment of assimilation, reaction and dialogue, the continuation and renewal of Clebsch and Jaekle's four strands of pastoral care: guiding, sustaining, healing and reconciling. These strands overlap in all aspects of pastoral care, including the three more structured forms of spiritual direction, counselling and the healing ministries. I put these activities in this order partly for historical reasons and partly to emphasise that advice and counselling seek to move towards healing and wholeness in those they aim to help. We will discuss these three dimensions of pastoral care in the next chapter.

Questions for Discussion

1. Discuss how, within the group's experience, the four strands of pastoral care – guiding, reconciling, sustaining and healing – are practised in the Church today. Reflect on, and pray about, ways that the balance between these strands could be improved.

2. Share your understanding and appreciation of any secular approach to counselling that you have had contact with. Discuss where each approach seems to fit in with an emphasis on patterns of behaviour, the exploration of the past, the importance of the person in effecting change, or the need for resources beyond ourselves (see pp. 48–51).

3. If any of you have received training in caring and counselling through a local church or other Christian body, try to discern whether the attitude towards secular approaches was one of rejection, unthinking assimilation or the desire to engage in dialogue (see pp. 48–51).

4. In Galatians chapter six, Paul urges his readers to 'carry each other's burdens' and so 'fulfil the law of Christ' (v.2). (The latter seems to refer to Jesus' 'new commandment' of John 13:24: 'Love one another'.) The sense here is of helping one another with life's heavy loads, the sort that weigh us down. Paul also writes that 'each one should carry his own load' (v.5), the manageable backpack of individual daily responsibility. Discuss how you can respond to both these instructions without, on the one hand, being swamped by others' needs or, on the other hand, becoming too self-contained. Try to give examples of success or failure in this area from your own experience.

Personal Reflection

Jesus was aware of his own needs and was able to ask others for help. He said to the Samaritan woman, 'Will you give me a drink?' (John 4:7); he regularly withdrew to the home of Mary, Martha and Lazarus just outside Jerusalem, and valued their friendship;

in Gethsemane, he said to Peter, James and John, 'My soul is overwhelmed with sorrow to the point of death. Stay here and keep watch' (Mark 14:34).

Reflect on a time when you sought the help of others. Maybe you were disappointed with the response. Ask yourself whether you made your need reasonably clear or whether you were too fearful or proud to seek help straightforwardly. Perhaps the fault lay in the potential helper who was too busy, felt threatened by your approach, or lacked insight and compassion. Spend some time praying about this, asking God's forgiveness for any failure on your part to be a burden-sharer and, where appropriate, telling God you forgive others for not being adequate burden-bearers.

However, maybe your experience of being helped was a good one. You were taken seriously, listened to, lovingly challenged, gently encouraged. Thank God afresh for the care given and received and ask him for his help to live out what was learned.

Jesus was also readily available to meet the needs of others – whether old or young, rich or poor, powerful or powerless, healthy or diseased, dutiful or wayward. Reflect on a time when you responded to another, through hospitality, practical help, advice, visiting in home, hospital or prison, counselling, or simply listening. Perhaps your attempt to help bear their burdens was spurned or misunderstood, or you felt manipulated or taken advantage of in some way. Ask God to forgive any resentment or bitterness you might still hold.

Perhaps, though, the experience was essentially valuable and valued. Thank God for his strength and encouragement in your caring and commit the person helped to his continuing love and enabling.

Finally, reflect prayerfully on these words of Jean Vanier as he writes of the caring love of Jesus:

He comes to make us children of the Father,
revealing the Father's incredible tenderness and hope

for each one of us.
He comes to heal our wounded hearts
by entering into a relationship of love
with each one of us.
Then through this relationship of love,
this communion,
he teaches us to open up in a relationship of love
with other people.[24]

4

The Three Faces of Pastoral Care

Christ is the complete physician of our wounds.

Augustine

We have seen something of how, historically, the Church's pastoral care has been expressed through the functions of guiding, healing, sustaining and reconciling. We have noted the powerful influences of the four systems of secular psychology which, in offering a wide range of solutions for troubled humankind, have both paralleled and, in some quarters, usurped these pastoral functions. We have observed debate and dialogue amongst Christians and their secular colleagues in today's world of counselling and have witnessed attempts by the Church to recover its identity in the calling of pastoral care. Let us now consider how Christ, 'the complete physician', brings repair and restoration into our lives through three aspects of that pastoral care: spiritual direction, counselling and healing.

Spiritual Direction

Whereas counselling became a buzz-word from the 1950s, and a renewed interest in healing arose with the charismatic movement from the 1960s onwards, spiritual direction has had an increasingly wide following amongst Christians since the 1970s. Even so, its roots are ancient. Linked traditionally with the Spirit's gift of discernment (*diakrisis*), 'distinguishing between spirits' (1 Cor. 12:10), and with the spiritually mature, 'who by constant use have trained themselves to distinguish good from evil' (Heb. 5:14), spiritual direction is an important element in the history of pastoral care. Two early strands in this story are the non-judgmental guidance given by the Desert Fathers in Egypt, in the fourth century, and the spiritual advice offered by the 'soul-friend' in the context of Celtic Christianity, in the sixth century.[1]

People who have greatly influenced spiritual direction through history include Ignatius Loyola (c. 1491–1556), and his *Spiritual Exercises*; John of the Cross, whose *Dark Night of the Soul* portrayed the grievous, but ultimately illuminating, experience of God's apparent absence; Francis de Sales (1567–1622), whose gentle direction often took place through his letter-writing; Reginald Somerset Ward (1881–1962), an Anglican priest who devoted himself to a travelling ministry of guiding others; and Thomas Merton (1915–1968), the Trappist monk whose emphasis on solitude and contemplation was coupled with serving God in the everyday world.

What do we mean by spiritual direction? Some may have a vision of an austere, authoritarian and yet shadowy figure, sitting in his study or monastic cell, and visited with some trembling for the confession of sin and resulting penance. However much this picture may be true in certain contexts, the revival of direction today has quite a different feel to it. Authoritarianism and elitism are out: friendship and a sense of fellow-pilgrimage are in. Kenneth Leech indicates this new emphasis, when he writes:

What then is spiritual direction? It is a relationship of friendship in Christ between two people by which one is enabled, through the personal encounter, to discern more clearly the will of God for one's life, and to grow in discipleship and in the life of grace.[2]

This 'friendship in Christ' (also known as soul-friendship, spiritual friendship or spiritual guidance) is marked by being freely sought by the directee; it is open to being discontinued and it has an agenda as wide as is deemed necessary for 'discerning the will of God'. Gordon Jeff, in his *Spiritual Direction for Every Christian*, points to the danger of elitism in this form of pastoral care, whereby an aura of mystique and 'specialness' surrounds what looks, from the outside, like an intense and collusive relationship. He asks:

> Is it totally unrealistic to suggest that every single Christian would benefit from talking over – even if only once a year – how they were getting on in their Christian pilgrimage, and especially in their direct relationship with God which we call prayer?[3]

In raising this question, Jeff exposes the heart of what spiritual direction should be about. Without denying that there are those, often in positions of leadership and battling perhaps with loneliness or a particular assault on their faith, who especially need the space provided by wise and regular direction, there is surely a wider context for most, if not all, of God's people. Here, once more, we are in the realm of our 'one-anotherness' in Christ. We see the comprehensiveness of a Christian ministry which seeks the maturity, an averred aim of spiritual direction, of all believers in these words of the apostle Paul:

> We proclaim him, admonishing and teaching everyone with all wisdom, so that we may present everyone perfect (mature) in Christ. To this end I labour, struggling with all his energy, which so powerfully works in me. (Col. 1:28–29)

Teleios, the word used here and elsewhere by Paul, can be variously translated as perfect, complete, adult or mature. This sense of completeness or maturity is the declared goal of all pastoral care, and it is an enterprise not only for the individual but for the Church corporately, 'so that the body of Christ may be built up . . . and become mature, attaining to the whole measure of the fulness of Christ' (Eph. 4:12–13).

We will look more fully at the nature of spiritual and psychological maturity in chapter seven but, for the moment, let it suffice to say that spiritual direction is, supremely, concerned with the concept of becoming more Christlike. As has often been argued, soul-friendship is primarily committed to the process of growth towards Christian maturity, whereas, as we shall see, counselling is often focused on the problems that block or stunt that growth. Spiritual direction, involving perhaps a monthly contact initially and later one every quarter or so, is a more structured form of caring, akin, in its commitment to Christian growth, to the wider concepts of pastoring, shepherding or discipling. All are attempts to respond to God's challenge to 'one-anotherness', although all are equally susceptible to an authoritarianism which forgets the Master's call to servanthood.

Finally, we cannot leave this brief section on spiritual direction without an understanding of the term commonly associated with it: spirituality. This word, first used pejoratively for a rarified form of piety in Catholic France in the seventeenth century, has become widely used in recent decades for any natural, human yearning to find meaning and significance beyond the self. This yearning may, of course, be expressed through almost any belief system, ranging from monotheistic religions like Judaism and Islam, through Eastern mysticism to pre-Christian world-views, resurfacing in the New Age Movement, and the occult. David G. Benner has defined Christian spirituality quite simply as 'a state of deep relationship with God made possible through faith in Jesus Christ and the indwelling Holy Spirit'.[4]

It is as we reflect on this 'deep relationship with God' that we see that the idea of spirituality is intrinsic to many other ways of describing the profounder aspects of Christian experience, as seen in Thomas à Kempis' *The Imitation of Christ*, Brother

Lawrence's *The Practice of the Presence of God*, Jeremy Taylor's *The Rule and Exercise of Holy Living*, John Bunyan's *The Pilgrim's Progress*, William Law's *Serious Call to a Devout and Holy Life* and Hannah Whitall Smith's *The Christian's Secret of a Happy Life*. Most understandings of spirituality include the idea of growth and change, what Paul Evdokimov, the Orthodox theologian, calls 'Christification'.[5] The Bible is, of course, full of imagery for the process and progress of our relating to Christ: we are to 'press on towards the goal to win the prize for which God has called (us) heavenwards in Christ Jesus' (Phil. 3:14); to 'grow up into him who is the Head, that is, Christ' (Eph. 4:15); and thus, through the work of the Spirit, we will be 'transformed into his likeness with ever-increasing glory' (2 Cor. 3:18). And it is spiritual direction at its best that will be open to the Holy Spirit's cultivating work in our lives. As David Benner puts it:

> Genuine Christian spirituality is like a delicate flower. We must care for it with extreme sensitivity, ever guarding that we do not allow others to trample it. It must be watered and fed; but its growth cannot be rushed nor manipulated. The direction our spiritual development takes must remain outside the control of others as well as ourselves. We will, therefore, from time to time experience anxiety about where these developments are taking us. But the Christian need not fear, because the spirit within is not some unknown or alien spirit but the Holy Spirit, the Spirit of Jesus whom we know.[6]

Counselling

Contemporary suspicion towards counselling is illustrated in a *Punch* cartoon, where a nervous Humpty-Dumpty is seen poised over a huge frying pan, with the caption, 'Trust me – I'm a Counsellor!' The roots of this suspicion are many and various, and include the belief that counselling sees itself as the panacea for all human ills and that the counsellor is a self-promoting semi-professional who sets himself up as priest or guru.

We need to understand that counselling, although it can claim too much for itself, is best viewed in the wider context of human caring. As we have already noted, it emerged in its present form from the 1930s onwards, was strongly influenced by the rise of the secular psychologies, and was received variously by the Church, with rejection, assimilation or dialogue. Where Christians have evaluated this development in the light of Scripture and its common grace theology, and discerned thereby what is good, bad and indifferent, counselling can be seen as a legitimate aspect of pastoral care.

Before we go further, we need to state some sort of definition of counselling, as we did for pastoral care in the last chapter. This is a notoriously difficult enterprise due to the wide range of assumptions, aims and techniques that have formed and modified the counselling movement.[7] I believe that the most appropriate way of describing counselling needs to incorporate the more relevant perspectives that the Bible gives on human nature and its needs. Not surprisingly, if we believe in a God who reveals himself through the created order, we find that a great deal of psychological research accords well with these emphases.[8] Keeping in mind the biblical view that we are living unities, often out of key with God, others and the world around, and that, during times of special difficulty, we may need enabling through another person, I would like to put forward the following definition. *Counselling is that activity which aims to help others towards constructive change in any or every aspect of life through a caring relationship, which has agreed boundaries and lays due emphasis on psychological mechanisms.*

Although we shall be unpacking this definition throughout the rest of this book (for instance, 'constructive change' in chapters seven and eight and the 'caring relationship' in chapters six and nine), it is worth sketching in briefly here some of the scriptural dimensions that have helped to shape it.

Any or Every Aspect of Life

We have already seen, in chapter two, that we have been created as 'living unities' and so any form of counselling which seeks to be true to biblical insight will acknowledge the indivisibility of the human beings it tries to help. This does not mean that every encounter in counselling will include a panoramic survey of all aspects of human life, but rather that, in dealing with any part, the whole will be kept in mind. Where, for example, the focus is on the behavioural and occupational, the social, relational, emotional, physical, psychological, aesthetic, moral and spiritual dimensions will also be watched for. Where, say, counselling centres on the behaviour of a client, whose milk-round in the early morning exposes him to the amorous intentions of a particular married woman, the issue is unlikely to be resolved purely in terms of varying his route or wearing a disguise! It is more than probable that the client's emotional turmoil, stress-related tiredness, the tension created in relating to his own wife and children, his increasing temptation to reciprocate his customer's interest and the disruption of his prayer life, will all figure somewhere in the helping process.

Of course, spiritual direction and counselling often overlap. Because spiritual direction focuses on the individual's progress as a Christian, and because Christ seeks lordship over every domain, soul-friendship will at times find itself dealing with psychological dilemmas and emotional blocks. Conversely, counselling, being open to 'every aspect of life', will sometimes shift from, say, examining the defence mechanism of projecting blame on to a mother to challenging the client to forgive and accept forgiveness. Depending on the personal qualities, training and experience of the director or counsellor, there may be the need for referral where either the psychological or spiritual dimensions, respectively, come to predominate. There is, however, a need for caution since the helping relationship, once established, may be the best milieu for continuing to work through the emerging difficulties. Alastair V. Campbell, in his *Paid to Care?*, has the right balance when he questions the rigid adherence to 'correct' technique in the face of untidy human need. He writes:

> . . . all helping of individuals must transcend theoretical understanding by meeting the particular . . . This, indeed, is what counselling achieves when it becomes, in the hands of an experienced practitioner, more than a mere technique woodenly repeated.[9]

Agreed Boundaries

All the best working relationships have boundaries that are agreed on – either explicitly or implicitly. In the covenant between God and his people, for instance, the understanding is made explicit: 'Now if you obey me fully and keep my covenant, then out of all nations you will be my treasured possession' (Exod. 19:5). The marriage contract is also made openly before witnesses, although there can often be more hidden elements, such as the assumption that the husband will be the breadwinner. In friendship there is a mutual commitment which is commonly left unexpressed, especially in Western society.

In counselling, however, there is a fundamental need for at least some discussion about the limits and extent of the anticipated relationship. This is required because the process of counselling has to have some sort of shape if it is to avoid either just petering out or continuing for ever! For a client to pluck up the courage to see a counsellor, but never quite know what the overall plan is, can be unsettling and even destructive.

Heeding, then, Campbell's warning against 'mere technique woodenly repeated', 'agreed boundaries' need to be established at an early stage in counselling. Client and helper discuss such practicalities as the number and duration of sessions, as well as the overall aim of the proposed counselling. It is important that these plans are agreed on by both parties and yet are also seen to be flexible and open to further debate. The counselling contract is designed to free the helping process rather than tie it to obsessive routine.

Psychological Mechanisms

It is important to remind ourselves that the psychological is as crucial an aspect as any in our image-bearing humanity. The term 'psychology' and its variants have their root in the Greek word *psyche*, meaning life, breath, soul or spirit and personified as Psyche, Cupid's lover, whose beauty outshone that of Venus. It is symptomatic of Western world-views that the word's derivatives commonly embrace the concept of 'mind', rather than 'soul' or 'spirit' – a psychologist has been defined, for example, as someone who goes to the Folies Bergères to look at the audience! The *Shorter Oxford English Dictionary* defines psychology more prosaically as 'the science of the nature, functions and phenomena of the human soul or mind'. Here we can see that psychology is a comprehensive field which surveys the essence of our human nature in terms of our thoughts, hopes, feelings, dreams, intuition, imagination, decision making, actions and patterns of behaviour. This rich terrain is the heartland of the paracletic ministry of counselling.

With respect to psychological mechanisms, would-be counsellors need at least a measure of understanding of the inner conflicts, mixed motives, insecurities and resistances to change that govern the lives of many of those they will counsel, as well as their own. In fact, these two perspectives are inseparable: true self-understanding is impossible without genuine relating to others, and a valid appreciation of other people is hamstrung where there is little or no self-awareness. Such insights come by many routes: through relationships, reflecting on life's ups and downs, suitable training in counselling, regular supervision or spiritual direction and, above all, through a life that cultivates a listening ear – to God, others and the self. One of the aims of this book is to help the reader with this dual understanding.

Listening to God - others - self -

Attentive listening, with an appreciation of psychological mechanisms, is the hallmark of all effective caring – not least in the related realms of counselling and psychotherapy. These two terms are readily confused and it is worth saying something here to try to untangle the muddle. Historically, counselling has been associated most with the personalism of humanistic psychology, and psychotherapy with the psychoanalytic tradition and existentialism. As we saw in chapter three, transpersonalism has more recently made inroads into both disciplines. However, these broad influences do not give us hard and fast distinctions between these two forms of helping others. To add to the difficulty, in the United States, the words 'counselling' and 'psychotherapy' are often used interchangeably, as in the influential book *Towards Effective Counseling and Psychotherapy* by Charles B. Truax and Robert R. Carkhuff, published in 1967.

It is my own conviction that there is a great deal of overlap between what is clearly recognised as counselling and what is acknowledged to be psychotherapy. Referring back to our definition of counselling on page 63, we can say that both activities stress the aim of 'constructive change' and the central nature of the helping relationship. It is in psychotherapy, however, that 'agreed boundaries' and 'psychological mechanisms' tend to be given greater prominence. Further, there is, in psychotherapy, a tendency to emphasise the role of the therapist, including his or her expertise, training in a particular methodology, or association with an appropriate institution, such as a hospital, clinic or suite of consulting rooms. In contrast, counselling is frequently more 'client-centred', to use Carl Rogers' phrase, although it pays increasing attention to questions of training, supervision and accreditation. One recent paper, in the context of psychiatry, gives the above emphasis in its definition of psychotherapy:

Psychotherapy is the treatment of a patient by psychological processes in the setting of a patient-therapist relationship in

Existentialism –

which the involvement of the therapist is a clearly recognised factor. No specific theoretical orientation is implied, nor are specialist behavioural treatments specifically excluded.[10]

Healing

Both spiritual direction and counselling, which seek to aid the maturing process through guiding, reconciling and sustaining, need to be open to the fourth strand of pastoral care mentioned by Clebsch and Jaekle: healing. This ministry, with deep roots in the story of God's dealings with afflicted humanity, has re-emerged during the twentieth century as 'an idea whose time has come'. The climate of change which has fostered this development has come about through a variety of influences. These include the achievements of Western medicine, the founding of the World Health Organisation after the devastation of the Second World War, the rise of psychologies which emphasise the whole person, a growing interest in 'alternative' treatments, a coming together of medical and pastoral thinking and practice through such bodies as the Institute of Religion and Medicine, and, with a new openness to the miraculous, the emergence of the charismatic, renewal and (through the influence of John Wimber and others) 'third wave' movements in the Churches.[11]

What, then, is meant by the term 'healing'? We read in the Bible that God is Healer and see in its pages numerous examples of his healing words and actions, expressed most clearly in the compassionate acts of Jesus, who healed 'every disease and sickness among the people' (Matt. 4:23). This divine, healing activity of Christ was comprehensive (including such chronic and 'incurable' conditions as blindness, deafness, muteness, deformity and paralysis), immediate and complete – in a word, miraculous. Even so, behind the spectacular was a Creator God who had made living beings with inbuilt mechanisms for healing and recovery and had provided, within the plant, animal and mineral worlds, rich resources for bringing health. This God has no 'splits' in his restoring work, whether through natural processes, as in the case of Job's calamitous skin disease, the help of medical aid, as with Isaiah's fig poultice (2 Kgs 20:7), or the ministrations of Jesus and his followers, bringing wholeness by touch or word to maimed lives.

In order to reach an understanding of the term 'healing' in relation to pastoral care, let us briefly consider it under three headings: healing and wholeness; healing and others; and healing and suffering.

Healing and Wholeness

Healing, as I have already indicated, can be equated with wholeness. Some of the relevant Greek words used in the New Testament bear this out: for example, *sozo*, meaning to save, preserve or rescue, indicates deliverance from evil and the bringing of wholeness; and *hygiano* carries more weight than our somewhat insipid word 'hygiene', with its picture of scrubbed finger nails and clean kitchens, and points to a profound healing of the whole person. Morris Maddocks has linked this latter term with the Hebrew word *shalom*, 'peace be with you', and its relevance to healing: he writes that this Old Testament greeting means 'well-being in the widest sense of the word – prosperity, bodily health, contentedness, good relations between nations and men, salvation'.[12]

Without denying the force of these biblical words, however, the idea of 'wholeness' in the here and now has its pastoral dilemmas, for it is readily taken to mean completeness, or even perfection. There is no doubt that Jesus brought wholeness to the woman, faint and anaemic after twelve years of recurring haemorrhage, when he said, 'Take heart, daughter, your faith has healed (*sozo*) you' (Matt. 9:22). Her wretched illness was cured instantly, her vitality and motivation restored, and, we are to understand, she had a new peace with God and a new calling to live a life of thankfulness and service. However, the 'wholeness' she received cannot have meant that she was never ill or upset again, that she never aged, never fell out with friends or family, or needed God's further forgiveness. Surely we need to understand that her healing brought a dramatic and far-reaching change for the better in every aspect of her being, but, like (all) whom Christ has touched, she was now on a continuing journey towards a fully realised wholeness, an ultimate healing. As Paul writes, in the context of the bodily resurrection, 'Though outwardly we are wasting away, yet inwardly we are being renewed day by day' (2 Cor. 4:16).

We need, I believe, to see the interweaving of salvation and healing. In the end, they are all of a piece. And, just as we can talk of having been saved, being saved and that we will be saved, we are truest to the Bible when we declare that, through Christ, we have been made whole, we are being made whole and we will be made whole. It is where we have this overview of wholeness as state, process and goal that we can avoid some of the pitfalls which lie in wait within the various healing ministries. On the one hand, we will avoid extravagant claims of cure where the evidence of change is lacking and, on the other hand, we will rejoice where the ill are made well, the oppressed delivered and the troubled unburdened – foretastes, *hors d'oeuvres* of the coming, glorious banquet for redeemed humanity.[13]

Healing and Others

Healing cannot take place in a vacuum: the road to wholeness inevitably involves others. Whether it involves sudden and dramatic physical change, the gradual and steady improvement of troublesome symptoms, the inner healing of deep emotional scars or the restoration of healthy thinking and attitudes to a disturbed mind, the discovery of well-being cannot be in isolation. Others – friends, family, fellow-believers, even foes – are caught up with the event or process, responding with delight, cynicism, support, incredulity, encouragement or dismay. People's reactions are complex and there is a sense in

which the healing of someone brings a crisis to the onlookers
and, in keeping with the Greek idea of *krisis* as judgment, a
moment of decision.

We see such a crisis, for example, in the story of the paralysed
man described in Mark 2:1–12. Although the paralytic is the
recipient of forgiveness and a spectacular healing, Jesus, and
the response of others to him, is in a sense the centrepiece
of the scene. We see here not only a crisis, a judgment, in
the life of the incapacitated man but also a point of challenge to
all present: the four friends who lowered him into the crowded
room come with faith in the compassion and power of Jesus;
the 'teachers of the law', in spite of their professional mask,
react with hidden rage and accusation at this rabbi who claims
he can forgive sins; and the crowd, thronging the house and its
approach, respond with amazement and praise to the God who
heals. Robert Lambourne, medical practitioner and theologian,
has particularly stressed the way in which healing becomes a
crisis for others; he wrote:

> The healings . . . were not merely effective signs in which
> Christ and the healed man were the sole actors, but effective
> signs in which all present took part, and not least those who
> scoffed. They were *public* effective signs.[14]

If, then, we are to be true to Scripture in the healing ministries, as well as in spiritual direction and counselling, we
need to keep in mind the wider context of people's lives.
This awareness should not only include the friends and family
of the one who seeks a new level of health but the further
horizons of living conditions, the workplace, the social environment and other healing agencies. A great deal of illness,
both physical and mental, relates to poor housing, overcrowd-
ing, financial difficulties, homelessness, hazards at work, being
out of favour with the authorities and inept levels of care in
the community. Here there is a call to a greater knowledge
of and concern about social issues and a better degree of

co-operation between the caring professions, voluntary and statutory agencies and the local churches. Stephen Pattison, a pastoral theologian now working in community health, lays down the challenge:

> Faith is not primarily passive waiting upon God. It is the active struggle for healing and wholeness amidst the socio-political complexities, ambiguities and conflicts of an industrialised society which makes many people sick and deprives them of real hope in the future. With our major secular health care institutions under threat, there has never been a more important time for faithful Christian healing of a kind which is prepared to act within situations of conflict.[15]

Healing and Suffering

It is all part of the reality of our image bearing and fallenness that the themes of healing and suffering interweave. However we understand the problems of evil, affliction and disaster, the Bible makes clear that we have a God who not only heals but also permits and uses suffering. We see this twin perspective when Job says this of God: 'For he wounds, but he also binds up; he injures, but his hands also heal' (Job 5:18).

There will always be mystery here and theologians and philosophers still wrestle with the seeming inconsistency of a God who, though all-loving and all-powerful, permits evil.[16] We saw in chapter two something of the realities of the human bid for independence from God, shifting life's focus from obedient image bearing to a disobedient idolatry. However we understand the links between the Adversary's seductive ways, human rebellion and the unfolding story of violence, disease and disaster, we have to accept the reality of suffering as part of the way things are in this fallen world.

We cannot deny, of course, that much affliction is self-imposed, whether wilfully (where heavy smokers knowingly risk a range of lung diseases), unwittingly (where a woman, unprotected and in ignorance, sleeps with her AIDS-infected husband) or out of necessity (where a village is rebuilt on the fertile flanks of a sleeping volcano because there is nowhere else to go). Yet the suffering of those whose afflictions bear little or no link with personal sin or folly is a vast human dilemma: the baby born with gross handicaps as the result of a chance virus caught by the mother; the man or woman whose life-long tendency to depression is genetically determined; the fit young person rendered immobile by a spinal injury from a diving accident.

Those of us who suffer from long-term debility which is not self-inflicted may have special difficulty in accepting the continuing curtailments involved. In the late 1970s, I experienced the beginning of many years of serious visual handicap, a complication of longstanding diabetes. After eight months of blindness, relieved by major surgery on my operable right eye, I emerged into a newly visible world, eager to re-acquaint myself with friends, family, books and garden. There was just one snag: I did not feel well enough to enjoy this visual feast.

One month before, Simon, our son, and I had eaten some soft cheese he had brought back from rural France as a present, and now we were both ill with what later proved to be brucellosis. Simon fortunately fought off this debilitating condition over the next few months but, with my inadequate immune system, I succumbed to the chronic form of the disease. Blindness was now replaced by extreme weakness, joint aches, a dry cough and feverishness, which became familiar companions over the coming months and years.

By the autumn of 1979, Joy and I had come through a very demanding few years and we now had the prospect of a short holiday on Colonsay, one of the Inner Hebrides, off the west coast of Scotland. Although I was greatly weakened by the continuing brucellosis, at least I had had my one-eyed vision back for five months or so and we greatly looked forward to the peace and beauty of the island. God had been good to us in countless ways and a brief break would soon restore us for the winter ahead. Our first day was wet, the second fine and, for the third, we planned a visit to the northern coast, hopefully to see golden eagles. However, this was not to be, for I woke that morning to the grim realisation that I was blind once more. There had been a large fresh haemorrhage at the back of the sighted eye during my sleep. The combination now of continuing brucellosis and the reversion to blindness seemed bleak and forbidding.

The shock for Joy and myself was considerable. Angry and tearful, we walked out on the local moors, arm in arm. At first we were too stricken for words but, later that day, the inevitable questions were expressed: 'Why, God? Why, after blindness and brucellosis do we need a third trial? Haven't we already proved your power to keep in adversity? What is the point of this fresh restriction, just as we thought we were coming out of the tunnel?' In some ways the questions were pointless, for there could be no immediate answers, and yet they had to be asked. It was as we put our anger into words that God gradually stilled us and showed us once more the infinitely greater suffering that his Son had borne for us, as he embraced the sins and afflictions of fallen humanity on the cross. There was no explanation; we experienced instead an assurance that, amidst the interweaving of suffering and healing in our lives, Christ, who is both Healer and Suffering Servant, would be a present and loving companion.

God not only allows suffering within his redemptive plan, he experiences it too. As the Book of Isaiah puts it, predicting the passion of Christ:

He was despised and rejected by men,
a man of sorrows, and familiar with suffering.
Like one from whom men hide their faces
he was despised, and we esteemed him not. (Isa. 53:3)

In Jewish thinking, to suffer so must have meant that here was one culpable of the most heinous sins. 'Despised and rejected', he was receiving his just deserts. History and Christian under-standing have revealed that the promised Messiah was, in fact, receiving the 'just deserts' of a sinful and rebellious humanity. We can never measure the full horror of Christ's passion: the betrayal, the desertion, the mock-trial, the beatings, the impalation, the darkness of dereliction, the asphyxiating and lingering death. And, although that death was unique, a 'sin offering' for us, 'so that in him we might become the right-eousness of God' (2 Cor. 5:21), it seems that God continues to suffer with humankind in and through his people, who are called to 'the fellowship of sharing in his sufferings' (Phil. 3:10).

It is here that we are at the heart of pastoral care, for, within our caring and counselling, we need to recall that Christ the healer is also the 'man of sorrows', who has first-hand experience of suffering and continues to suffer in his Church. In that way, we will avoid an approach which sees a lack of faith or personal sin as the only limits on God's healing activity, and neglects the biblical reality of a theology of suffering while concentrating on a theology of healing. This mistaken emphasis is in danger of replacing the power of love with the love of power, as Tom Smail has pointed out. We can take his timely words to apply in every aspect of our paracletic minis-try, whether seeking spiritual maturity through soul-friendship, psychological growth through counselling, release from the dark forces of oppression or possession through deliverance, or physical health through healing. He writes:

We do indeed need a good theology of healing; but, if that is all we have, we shall be in danger of being left in disillusionment and disappointment. We must have a theology of suffering that can see God's weak but mighty love at work in continuing disablements of all kinds, reshaping people who are open to it into deep relationships with himself and with others, that come from shared suffering rather than from instant miracles . . . There is a kind of strength that has never been to Calvary and that is really weakness; there is a kind of weakness that the love of God shown at Calvary can turn into strength. [17]

Questions for Discussion

1. Discuss spiritual direction or soul-friendship. Members of the group might like to share one or two positive or negative aspects of direction from their own experience. Do you feel it is (a) desirable and (b) practical for every Christian to receive some degree of spiritual direction in their life with God? Discuss the pros and cons.

2. Attempt a definition of counselling agreed on by the whole group (the larger the group, the more difficult this enterprise!). Compare your definition with the one on page 63, asking which ingredients are indispensable.

3. Robert Lambourne has described Christ's healings as 'public effective signs'. Discuss stories of gradual or sudden healing, experienced either by members of the group or by others known to them (be sure to preserve confidences though). What relevance do these healings have for others – friends, family, at work and in the community?

4. Read Colossians 1:28–29 and Ephesians 4:11–16. What do these passages teach us about Christian maturity, individually and corporately? Discuss briefly what help spiritual direction, counselling and the healing ministries can be in this process.

5. Someone has written that God says, in effect, to the sufferer, 'If I were in your shoes, and you in mine, I would have difficulty praising you'. [18] Discuss the dilemmas of unanswered prayer for healing and continuing affliction in the light of Hebrews 12:2–3. The story of Paul's 'thorn in the flesh' (an unknown source of suffering) in 2 Corinthians 12:7–10 may be helpful here.

Personal Reflection

Find somewhere where you can sit comfortably and undisturbed, ideally for half-an-hour. If you can, it is probably best to sit upright in a firm chair as this aids concentration. Close your eyes for a few minutes and become aware of your breathing.

Sense the nearness of the Holy Spirit, and, as you breathe in slowly, be aware of his presence around you and within. Ask the Lord to speak to you and show you his love, as he tells you how to care for others. Read the story of the Good Samaritan in Luke 10:25–37 slowly two or three times. *meditation*

Imagine yourself into the story, either as a spectator or as one of the people mentioned.

Sense the heat beating down, the stillness of the air, the haze obscuring the dusty road winding down ahead and the rough, rocky terrain on either side. This road is notorious for muggings and robbery, and you can almost smell the danger.

Set the scene in your mind as the drama begins to unfold. See the battered, naked figure slumped at the side of the road, a small flock of vultures already circling above. See the priest, and later the Levite, descending on the same route; see each figure in turn, clearly fearful for his own safety, pause at the body and then hurry on. Observe the Samaritan and his laden donkey approach, witness his concern, the dressing of the wounds and the pouring on of healing oil and wine. See his struggle to lift the limp body on to his beast of burden and watch the small group begin their slow journey to the nearest wayside inn.

Who do you most readily imagine yourself to be? A spectator, the wounded man, the priest or Levite, or the Samaritan? What feelings have come to you most readily? Fear, indifference, revulsion, pity, curiosity, a desire to help or be helped, or a feeling of helplessness?

Ask the Lord the question the lawyer asked: Who is my neighbour? In the story, the neighbour was the Samaritan, in other words the one who helped. Is God showing you anyone whom he may want to help you? Or, is there someone you know who needs your practical caring? Think across the barriers, because maybe there is someone of another culture, race, age-group, or level of fitness who can be a 'good neighbour' to you, or vice versa.

5

Care and Counsel in the Bible

The quiet words of the wise are more to be heeded than the shouts of a ruler of fools.

Ecclesiastes 9:17

There have always been those who provide a listening ear and a shoulder to cry on. Cicero, the Roman philosopher, declared, 'the soul that is sick cannot rightly prescribe for itself, except by following the instruction of wise men'.[1] In Shakespeare's day, there was an awareness that counsellors who are 'good' at their craft 'lacke no clients'.[2] In recent years, the psychiatrist Jerome Frank has pointed out the value of many in everyday life to whom the troubled readily turn, 'even strangers, especially if they occupy roles like that of the bartender, for example, which create the expectation that they will be good listeners'.[3]

Although, as far as I am aware, no bartenders grace the pages of Scripture, we do meet a range of callings whose task is to understand people's hopes and needs, and to mediate God's care and challenge to them. As we saw in chapter three, there are, according to Jacob Firet (see p. 43), three main strands through which God speaks – proclamation, teaching and consolation – and, though the roots of pastoral care lie primarily in the 'consolation' of *paraklesis*, all three contribute to meeting human need. Although the bartender, or the stranger in the train or bus, may provide the anonymous listening we crave, usually there will be little in the way of godly insight to be offered. In contrast, we find within the unfolding story of God's dealings with his people the emergence of prophet, priest, wise one and shepherd. We will look at each of these in turn, showing how each role was fulfilled in the life and work of Jesus Christ, and how these four callings influence pastoral care and counselling.

The Prophet

The twin call of the prophet was to warn of personal, communal or national judgment and to give promise of restoration and renewal. Jeremiah, for example, predicted the imminent downfall and captivity of God's people ('All Judah will be carried into exile, carried completely away' [Jer. 13:19]) and, in generations to come, their return to the Promised Land ('I will bring my people . . . back from captivity and restore them' [Jer. 30:3]). The warning note in such messages was not gladly received and to be a prophet was a lonely and exacting vocation, often involving isolation, misunderstanding and persecution. Seeing visions, having and sharing disturbing dreams, acting out street dramas and calling the people to repentance were not activities that made or kept friends – and accusations of eccentricity and irrelevance were the order of the day. John Goldingay has written of the cost for the one who proclaims God's prophetic word:

> It means accepting the tension of a twofold identification, with God in his anguish and indignation, and with Israel in her anguish and high calling. It means to stand boldly in confrontation with men, without ever being quite able to prove that the words which you declare are ones which you have overheard in Yahweh's council.[4]

It is in Jesus that we meet *the* prophet, anticipated in the promise

anguish   indignation – God
anguish   high calling – Israel

given to Moses: 'I will raise up for them a prophet like you from among their brothers; I will put my words in his mouth . . .' (Deut. 18:18).[5] Jesus himself knew that he was more than a prophet – declaring 'now one greater than Jonah is here' (Matt. 12:41) – for he not only warned of judgment, he came with the authority to judge; and he not only foretold restoration and renewal, he came to effect them. We see Jesus – empowered by the Spirit, the hallmark of the true prophet – bringing glad tidings to the needy, in fulfilment of Isaiah 61:1–2 (judgment, though predicted in the original prophecy – 'the day of vengeance of our God' – is, for the time being, to be held back):

'The Spirit of the Lord is on me, because he has anointed me to preach good news to the poor. He has sent me to proclaim freedom for the prisoners and recovery of sight for the blind, to release the oppressed, to proclaim the year of the Lord's favour'. (Luke 4:18–19)

The prophetic element in Christ's encounters – as he declares God's words, challenges, confronts and calls to repentance and new beginnings – can be observed now, not only in the pulpit but also within pastoral care, wherever spiritual direction, counselling and healing are being carried out in faithfulness to the God who speaks his word into our everyday lives.

The particular stress given to the prophetic dimension tends to vary between different sectors of pastoral care. In fact, as we shall see in chapter nine, we can legitimately use the term 'prophetic counselling' of Christian methodologies which concentrate on the cognitive and behavioural (see, also, figure 3 on p. 149). Such approaches tend to focus on wrong patterns of thinking and behaving and, as a result, emphasise the challenge of Scripture's call to repent and live obedient lives. All sectors of pastoral care, however, where they seek to be true to biblical revelation, will, at times, include the prophetic perspective. This is most faithful to the Bible's portrait of the prophet where warning and promise, challenge

Repentance – New beginnings

and hope, all prompted by the Holy Spirit, are held in balance.

The story of Jesus and the Samaritan woman in John 4 provides a clear example of the truly prophetic. Crossing boundaries of race, sex and gender, he takes time to build up a relationship of trust – admitting his thirst, debating with her, offering the hope of better things. Having won her attentive ear, he is then able to challenge her: 'Go call your husband and come back' (v. 16). He discerns the realities of her sexually promiscuous life and yet, amidst his challenge, continues to affirm her: 'You are right when you say you have no husband . . .' (v. 17). When Jesus confronts, he goes on loving – that is the way of the prophet within today's pastoral care and counselling.

The Priest

In the story of the Old Testament the priesthood emerged as an ancient company whose 'go-between' functions were many and various. They were to instruct the people in God's ways, 'so that they can listen and learn to fear the Lord your God and follow carefully all the words of this law' (Deut. 31:12); they were called to make sacrifices for the sins of Israel since they, especially the Levites, were set apart as God's chosen ones, for 'the Lord is their inheritance' (Deut. 10:9); and, further, they were to be consulted where difficult judgments were needed, the people being urged to 'be careful to do everything they direct you to do' (Deut. 17:10).

Jesus, of course, was not only more than a prophet, he was more than a priest, for he was *the* high priest. The life-long office of high priest, traced back to Aaron, reached its acme each year on the Day of Atonement when sacrifice was made and absolution declared for 'all the sins of the Israelites' (Lev. 16:34). Jesus was of a different order and bridged the gap between God and needy humanity perfectly: truly human and yet without sin, he could represent the people; fully God and yet incarnate, he could represent the Trinity. As the writer to the Hebrews declares:

> . . . because Jesus lives for ever, he has a permanent priest-hood. Therefore he is able to save completely those who come to God through him, because he always lives to intercede for them. Such a high priest meets our need – one who is holy, blameless, pure, set apart from sinners, exalted above the heavens. (Heb. 7:24–26)

Where we see Jesus mediating, reconciling, interceding, bringing forgiveness and identifying with fallen men and women, we meet the priestly aspect of pastoral care. Further, without denying the 'once and for all' uniqueness of Christ's high-priestly sacrifice, we find that the people of God are called to offer themselves in lives of service, lives that follow Jesus on the way to the cross, the way of suffering, rejection and dying to selfish ambition. Just as Israel was called to be a 'kingdom of priests and a holy nation' (Exod. 19:6), so the Church through the ages is declared to be 'a chosen people, a royal priesthood, a holy nation, a people belonging to God' (1 Pet. 2:9).

The self-giving, loving action that should arise out of this calling has many faces and many voices. Doris Pargeter is one such voice. A Londoner through and through, she featured on Radio 4 in 1987 in a programme called 'Doris's Boys', in which one told how she took mentally handicapped young men into her residential home. Her level of practical care included paying funeral expenses if one of them died, because 'they're now with Jesus'. In the face of local opposition to the inhabitants of 'Doris's Home', she said, 'There are more ways of crucifying people than putting them on a cross!'

There should be something of the compassionate 'go-between' element of Doris Pargeter's life in our own pastoral care. Ideally, the spiritual director, counsellor or healer acts as a bridgehead for the person in need to make advances on life's journey. Sometimes the carer is, in effect, the bridge too – helping the client to hear God afresh or, perhaps, for the first time. This bridging function has many aspects. Where the client has, for example, little sense of God's love, it may be the patient and caring attitudes of the counsellor that speak most powerfully of that higher level of loving. Just as the counsellor meets Christ in the lives of those who seek help, so the client meets Christ in the demeanour of the counsellor. As Robert Lambourne has put it, in the context of the ministry of healing, 'those concerned in it become little Christs',[6] representing and making plain the compassionate and health-giving nature of the Lord. This priestly role – mediating, bridge-building, opening up a meeting-place between God and people in need – while most evident in healing and spiritual direction, should be integral to all Christian care and counselling.

The Wise

Throughout the Near East in ancient times there grew up a class of 'wise ones' who were regarded as repositories of knowledge and wisdom. Amongst these was the 'wise woman from Tekoa' (2 Sam. 14) who braved King David to persuade him to allow the return of his rebellious son, Absalom. In time, the wise ones collected together a great store of 'wise sayings', culminating in the legendary wisdom of Solomon, who 'spoke three thousand proverbs' and whose songs 'numbered a thousand and five' (1 Kgs 4:32). The wisdom literature, including the canonical books of Job, the Psalms, Proverbs and Ecclesiastes, built up a library of succinct advice for successful living and profound reflection on the frustrations and mysteries of life. By the seventh century, three classes of pastoral carers were recognised, for Jeremiah's enemies talked of 'the teaching of the law by the priest', 'the word from the prophets' and 'counsel from the wise' (Jer. 18:18).

Supremely, of course, true wisdom belongs to God alone. In Proverbs 8, we see that wisdom is personified and declares her presence at the very heart of God's creative work: 'I was the craftsman at his side . . . rejoicing in his whole world and delighting in mankind' (Prov. 8:30–31). The New Testament takes up this theme and we can conclude that the wise one at the Creator's side is the Lord Christ, for 'He is the image of the invisible God, the firstborn over all creation' (Col. 1:15).

The Bible makes plain that this godly wisdom becomes available to those who, realising their unworthiness, acknowledge the greatness and goodness of God, for 'The fear of the Lord is the beginning of wisdom' (Ps. 111:10). This wisdom 'from above' contrasts sharply with the arrogance and pride of human knowingness. Freud, in a letter to an American colleague in 1915, wrote, 'Let me add that I am in no way in awe of the Almighty. If we ever met one another, it is rather I who should reproach Him, than he me.'[7]

But we do not need to point the finger at Freud, for none of us can begin to taste true wisdom unless we 'are in Christ Jesus, who has become for us wisdom from God' (1 Cor. 1:30). Let James remind us of the qualities of this godly perspective on life:

> . . . the wisdom that comes from heaven is first of all pure; then peace-loving, considerate, submissive, full of mercy and good fruit, impartial and sincere. (Jas 3:17)

Jesus himself, as we have already indicated, is *the* wise one – the one who taught the secrets of right living through parables and proverbial sayings, and of whom the people, amazed, asked, 'Where did this man get this wisdom and these miraculous powers?' (Matt. 13:54). We have the same sense of astonishment and awe in some of the messianic passages which anticipate Christ: for example, in the couplet 'Wonderful/Counsellor' (Isa. 9:6) and as the one on whom rests 'the Spirit of wisdom and of understanding, the Spirit of counsel and of power' (Isa. 11:2). Here is the one who possesses such treasures of wisdom and knowledge that good counsel can be found for every need and situation.

The followers of Christ are called not only to exhort as prophets and mediate as priests but to bring godly wisdom to their pastoral caring and counselling. The wise person who counsels needs the purity of motive, the willingness to learn, the thoughtfulness and the objectivity of the wisdom 'that comes from heaven'. Such a wise counsellor will be open to God's supernatural intervention in the Spirit's gifts of 'the message of wisdom' or 'the message of knowledge' (1 Cor. 12:8), as well as sharing the insights of 'wise sayings' and being prepared to tell and listen to life's stories. Alastair Campbell, in the context of pastoral care and counselling, touches on this last point as a vehicle of wise and loving caring:

> But the most simple and untrained person, perhaps a young child, perhaps a warm neighbour, can share in another's story. For listening to stories touches levels of feeling and experience which the intellect cannot entertain. By sharing in another's story one is 'being with' rather than 'doing to'.[8]

The prerequisite of godly wisdom is, of course, found in all sectors of pastoral care. The counsellor, even where the emphasis is primarily prophetic, needs to be able to listen carefully and speak out with a God-given discernment. As Paul puts it, in the context of prophetic declaration: 'We proclaim him, admonishing and teaching everyone *with all wisdom*' (Col. 1:28). Similarly, the spiritual director must be in tune with the Spirit's wisdom as he or she hears another's story and seeks to share something of the 'mind of Christ' (1 Cor. 2:16). As we have already noted, there is a close link in Old and New Testaments between wise counsel and the power to effect change, and this combined source of transformation is at its most explicit in the ministry of healing. Christ, 'the power of God and the wisdom of God' (1 Cor. 1:24), comes to deliver from the Enemy's grip and bring wholeness to every aspect of life.

The Shepherd

Underlying God's call to care through the prophetic word, priestly mediation and proverbial wisdom runs the theme of the shepherd. This image is of great importance in the development of ideas about Christian caring. Seward Hiltner spoke of the 'shepherding perspective' in the 1950s[9] and, more recently, Thomas Oden, in his *Pastoral Theology* (1983), has written of the shepherd as the 'pivotal analogy' within the leadership of Israel.[10] This analogy is, of course, implicit in the very term 'pastoral care'.

Although the literal meaning of 'pastor' and 'pastoral' is outmoded in the industrial West, the picture of shepherds with their flocks of sheep and goats was a familiar one throughout biblical times. God himself is seen as the Shepherd of his people, as we saw in chapter three (see p. 42), and he calls out leaders to act as 'under-shepherds' who will tend his flock. It seems that many of these carers in the old Testament failed profoundly in their pastoral duties and were condemned roundly by Jeremiah, Ezekiel and Zechariah:

> This is what the Sovereign Lord says: Woe to the shepherds of Israel who only take care of themselves! . . . You have not strengthened the weak or healed the sick or bound up the injured. You have not brought back the strays or searched for the lost. You have ruled them harshly and brutally. So they were scattered because there was no shepherd . . . (Ezek. 34:2–5)

This gross neglect of their charges by the under-shepherds gives way to the promise of a faithful Messiah, of whom the

Sovereign Lord says, 'I will place over them one shepherd . . . and he will tend them' (Ezek. 34:23), and whose calling leads to rejection and suffering (see Zechariah 11:7–11, 12:10 and 13:7). The fulfilment of this expectation is clear in Jesus' claim to be the Good Shepherd, who 'lays down his life for the sheep' (John 10:11).

Many of us are influenced by Victorian sentimentality in our mental image of a shepherd. We picture a tall, fair Anglo-Saxon figure swathed in freshly laundered and carefully arranged robes of some quality. He strikes a fine pose as he gazes, with exemplary eye contact, at his portrait painter, carved crook in one hand, a soulful-looking lamb gathered in the other and a collection of image-conscious, prime sheep grouped respectfully about his feet. In reality, the life of a shepherd is a tough and demanding one in any age and in any country: exposure to the elements, keeping wild animals and poachers at bay, the need for continual watchfulness, and the rigours of dipping, shearing and searching for lost sheep, all take their toll. In fact, by the time of Jesus, shepherds were not only seen as people of great physical endurance but as a class of ruffians, desperately poor and not to be trusted. One Jewish writing declared, 'No position in the world is as despised as that of the shepherd'.[11]

In the face of such disreputability it is all the more striking that Jesus takes up the metaphor for himself. But here we see the *Good* Shepherd, faithful and courageous in caring for his flock. We have a picture, drawn in great detail in John 10:1–18, which shows the intimate level of caring by the Messiah-Shepherd, and which informs and challenges us as under-shepherds. This shepherding perspective surfaces in pastoral care and counselling where we are called into a relating that is marked by elements of nurture, protection, trust and a preparedness to face adversity with courage. As for the prophet, priest and wise one, the model is Jesus. In his *Rediscovering Pastoral Care*, Alastair Campbell has written this:

. . . it is in the steadfast love of God incarnate in Jesus that

we see the shepherd's courage, not in the power and strength
of earthly leaders. The courage of Jesus has a quality to it that
is both strong and gentle. Above all, it is a courage *for others*,
not a courage for his own defence or aggrandisement.[12]

This 'courage for others' is at the heart of the shepherding
dimension of Christian caring. Although the roles of the prophet,
priest and wise one demonstrate concern for others, it is in the
role of shepherd, as we have seen, that the carer is most clearly
open to the relationship itself. Here we can point out certain
distinctions, for example, between the sectors of 'prophetic'
counselling and 'pastoral' counselling[13] (see figure 5 on p. 165).
Where the former stresses right thinking and behaviour, and
thus emphasises the 'admonishing' and 'exhorting' elements
of care, the latter concentrates on the relating within the
counselling process, and so tends to stress the 'consoling' and
'encouraging' strands. Both sectors, of course, are needed and
a great deal of Christian counselling which is relationship-based
is also open to declaring the prophetic word, 'speaking the truth
in love' (Eph. 4:15).

In summary, we can see that pastoral care and counselling
today, in seeking to be true to the biblical record, needs to
be aware of the complementary functions of prophet, priest,
wise one and shepherd. Although these functions are found
primarily in prophetic counselling, spiritual direction, the healing
ministries and pastoral counselling respectively, each branch of
pastoral care should, I believe, be both flexible in the emphasis
of its own ministry and prepared to respect, if not value, the
emphases of others.

Questions for Discussion

1. Try to sort the following caring activities under the headings 'prophet', 'priest', 'wise one' and 'shepherd': nurturing,
mediating, confronting, advising, exhorting, encouraging, challenging, guiding, consoling, warning, reconciling, reassuring,
instructing, giving insight, bringing forgiveness, comforting.

2. Using this list, take time to reflect and share those caring activities that you feel you are (a) *most* gifted with and (b) *least* gifted with.

3. Discuss the strengths and weaknesses of your fellowship, church or organisation with regard to the elements of exhortation and confrontation (the prophetic), forgiveness and reconciliation (the priestly), teaching and guidance (imparting of wisdom) and encouragement and nurture (the pastoral).

4. Spend a time of silent reflection or open prayer as you bring before God the work of caring in your sphere of influence. It has been said that when Jesus confronts, he goes on loving (see John 4 and the story of the woman of Samaria). Thank God for his firmness and tenderness towards us and ask him for whatever is lacking in the ministries of exhortation, reconciliation, wisdom or encouragement in your work for him.

Personal Reflection

In a number of places the Bible tells us to be still in God's presence. Try to find somewhere where you can be undisturbed for a while. Take time to allow a sense of stillness before God to develop. If your thoughts are crowded and distracting, jot the main ones down on a piece of paper for dealing with later. You may find it helpful to read and reread slowly the following verses:

Be still before the Lord, all mankind, because he has roused himself from his holy dwelling. (Zechariah 2:13)

'Be still, and know that I am God;
I will be exalted among the nations,
I will be exalted in the earth'. (Ps. 46:10)

[Jesus] got up, rebuked the wind and said to the waves, 'Quiet! Be still!' Then the wind died down and it was completely calm. (Mark 4:39)

> Be still before the Lord and wait
> patiently for him. (Ps. 37:7)

Ask God to speak to you in the stillness.

After a few minutes, reflect on the gifts, experience and skills he has given you with respect to caring and being cared for. Perhaps you are barely aware of these, or doubt your own worth to help others. Take your time, as you consider the main aspects of caring we have discussed in this chapter. Are you able to speak plainly and challenge others? Can you recall times when you have been a reconciler, a peacemaker? However diffident you may feel, are you sometimes valued for words of wisdom and the good advice you have been able to give? Are you an encourager, someone able to console the broken and grief-stricken – perhaps through silence, attentive listening or words of comfort?

Perhaps you have embarked on a training course in counselling, spiritual direction or the healing ministries, or maybe you have received training and have considerable experience in one or more of these fields. This could be a good moment to check out what brought you into the work of caring for others. Was it through someone else's help for your own conflicts and difficulties? Was it the result of an awareness of your gifts, or through a sense of God's calling? Was it originally a simple testing out of possibilities? Were you drawn by a need to be needed? Whatever the answers to questions like these, where are you now – in terms of motivation, effectiveness and a sense of direction? Do you have accountability to others in what you do – a supervisor, a director, a team of colleagues or some other support group? It could be helpful to write a short piece (say, one side of A4) about your story as a carer so far, using at least some of the above questions.

A Carer's Prayer

> Lord, when I need to challenge or confront
> may I do so with love
> When I need to bring together those at odds

may I do so with patience
When I need your words of wisdom
may I declare them as one who learns
When I need to comfort or console
may I do so as one who receives from you.

6

The Effective Counsellor

Good counsellors lacke no clients.

William Shakespeare

As a doctor in general practice and, later, in student health it was not that rare to be faced with criticism of a fellow-doctor, for patients sometimes have good cause to complain about the level of medical care they receive. My own approach on these occasions would be to listen and then try to put forward any likely extenuating circumstances. However, there were times when I found myself tacitly agreeing with the particular frustrations of certain patients. They had come to discuss their anxieties and, hopefully, unburden themselves, but had somehow, they felt, been fobbed off. There could have been many reasons for this: the doctor was extra tired; the patient was notoriously demanding; or there was, quite simply, a misunderstanding between them. It has to be said, however, that there are doctors, as with any other category of people, who do not seem to have it within them to pick up patients' questions and apprehensions in a way that clarifies and reassures. On the other hand, I well remember a colleague of mine whose listening skills were truly therapeutic. One middle-aged woman emerged, radiant with delight, after a half-hour consultation with this doctor and exclaimed, 'I've forgotten quite why I visited her . . . but she listened so well that I feel *much* better!'

Why is it that one member of the so-called caring professions seems to block people's genuine expression of need, whereas another is able to gauge a person's situation accurately and helpfully? As I have already indicated, there are many reasons for this variation, not least that the professional's skills may lie elsewhere – in administration, in the quick diagnosis of physical illness, in laboratory work. Personal attributes vary greatly and some people seem to be more health-giving than others. This question of the personality of the would-be helper is nowhere more pressing than in the realms of pastoral care and counselling.

It would be valuable now to ask what qualities are needed by the effective counsellor. Experience and research from the 1950s onwards tend to affirm and confirm the features noted from our examination of pastoral care in Scripture: that the caring qualities which characterise prophet, priest, wise one and shepherd also indicate the cardinal features of the effective counsellor. This should be no surprise as we acknowledge that the God of all truth is abroad in his world, revealing through common grace something of his ways in the lives of all people.

In our definition of counselling (see p. 63), we included the phrase 'the caring relationship', based on the premises that Christ calls us to love everyone, including our enemies, and that all caring is inevitably linked with what we have labelled 'one-anotherness.' There are, of course, many 'caring relationships' in life, including good neighbourliness, close friendship, the marriage bond, family affection and pastoral responsibility. As we have seen, the counselling relationship is defined in terms of 'agreed boundaries' and 'due emphasis on psychological mechanisms'. Inevitably, too, it is an asymmetrical relationship – unlike friendship, fellowship and marriage – for it is the meeting of two or more people in which it is understood that one party is primarily the helper, and the other the helped. As Martin Buber put it to Carl Rogers during an interchange on counselling:

A man coming to you for help. The essential difference between your role in this situation and his is obvious. He

comes for help to you. You don't come for help to him . . .
You are not equals and cannot be.[1]

Although there is some truth in Buber's view, a right understanding of counselling can offset some of this 'inequality',
for the qualities of the effective counsellor include his or her
accessibility as a person.

During the 1950s and early 1960s, the thriving professions of
counselling and psychotherapy reached a crisis point, as a result
of key figures like Hans Eysenck and Jerome Frank challenging
the very grounds for the existence of these professions.[2] In
short, they were arguing that these activities did not actually
work! This worrying conclusion provoked a spate of research
throughout the 1960s, which, still unnervingly, established that
at least some counsellors helped their clients, while others
seemed to be neutral in their effect, and a third category
managed to make people worse. There are few situations
which concentrate the mind more than the prospect that you
might be out of a job, and so the enquiry focused on what
characteristics in the counsellor or therapist influenced the
outcome of treatment. Although Carl Rogers had put his finger
on the key features of the 'good counsellor' as early as 1957,
it was the review published a decade later, *Towards Effective
Counseling and Psychotherapy*, by Charles Truax and Robert
Carkhuff, that brought together the clearest appraisal of the
qualities needed, the so-called 'core conditions' of the counselling relationship: 'genuineness', 'non-possessive warmth' and
'accurate empathy'.[3]

Genuineness

The word 'genuine' in everyday life implies validity and
authenticity. We might say to a guest who enquires of the
coffee we offer, 'No, it's not "instant". It's the genuine thing.
I ground the coffee beans myself this morning' or, to a shop
assistant, 'Is that jacket genuine leather? Is this dress genuine

silk?' One of the greatest accolades we can give is to say of someone, 'John is completely authentic in his care for others' or, 'Mary is absolutely genuine'. Genuineness, or authenticity, points to articles or people being what they seem to be. Gerard Egan summarises this quality as follows:

> Genuine people are at home with themselves and therefore can comfortably be themselves in all their interactions. This means that they do not have to change when they are with different people – that is, they do not constantly have to adopt new roles in order to be acceptable to others.[4]

This definition by Egan indicates two aspects of genuineness that are crucial within the counselling relationship: congruence and transparency.

Congruence

Congruence, the somewhat ugly word coined by Carl Rogers and others, is the quality of inner consistency in which counsellors can 'be themselves'. The idea is linked with the concept of identity that we looked at in chapter two (see pp. 30–37) and, in turn, implies both self-awareness (that we see ourselves straight) and self-respect (that we value what we see).

This need to 'see ourselves straight' is picked up by the apostle Paul in Romans 12:3, where he writes:

> For by the grace given me I say to every one of you: Do not think of yourself more highly than you ought, but rather think of yourself with sober judgment, in accordance with the measure of faith God has given you.

Behind the phrase, 'think of yourself with sober judgment' lies the Greek word *sophron*, made up from *sos*, meaning safe or sound, and *phren*, 'the heart as the seat of the passions'.[5] We are to demonstrate 'sound-heartedness' as we assess ourselves, thinking soberly, reasonably and with restraint.

It is important, though, to see the immediate context of this exhortation, for Paul writes of the 'grace given' as the spur of his words and the 'faith given' as the grounds for sober thought. Here, we are reminded once more that self-knowledge and God-knowledge are inextricably linked, that the route to congruence, self-awareness and self-respect lies within the bounds of listening to God. The prayer of the psalmist signposts the way:

> Search me, O God, and know my heart;
> test me and know my anxious thoughts.
> See if there is any offensive way in me,
> and lead me in the way everlasting.
> (Ps. 139:23–24)

Transparency

Genuineness, to be effective, has to go places: it is useless if it stands aloof and alone. And so, the congruence, or sense of inner consistency, that God can increasingly bring into our lives, needs to flow outwards – both for its own vitality and to give life to others. It would be of little use to be genuine as a mother, friend or lover if there was no natural outlet into mothering, friendship or loving. An essential part of all valuable relationships is that the genuineness is *seen for what it is*. A declaration, 'Everyone tells me that my mother is completely genuine, but I've never spotted it!', would be a cry of cynicism or despair.

In the context of caring and counselling, we refer to this mediation of genuineness and self-consistency as *transparency*. Here there is a need for a correct balance between congruence and a degree of openness. Some who counsel may come across as frank and honest, but we, as clients, are made uncertain because we sense a lack of self-awareness and integration in the carer. It can be next to impossible to open up to someone like this, someone who is clearly ill at ease, seems full of unresolved conflict and is unable to 'ring true'. Other counsellors may be genuine, self-aware and consistent, but we would never know! They seem detached, even cold, and the sort of people they really are remains closed to the client. We cannot share ourselves with them for they will share nothing of themselves with us.

There is a fine line to be drawn, for a counsellor who is authentic and reasonably integrated could be dangerously persuasive or impossibly tedious if he or she used counselling sessions to tell all! I am not arguing that it is never appropriate for counsellors to share something of their own stories. In my own experience, having listened carefully to the client, there have been times when a confession of a parallel difficulty in my own life or a sharing of an encouraging experience have been just what was needed. I am pointing out, rather, the danger of the counsellor who shares too readily, blocking the client's need to tell his or her own tale in considerable detail. There are few worse situations in counselling than when someone in need has, perhaps for the first time, an opportunity to unburden and is met too readily with, 'Oh, that's quite a coincidence! Let me tell you what happened to *me* the other day . . .' Each individual's situation and story are quite unique and interruptions from a counsellor, who is high on inner consistency and transparency but low on self-restraint and listening skills, may mean that the client is never fully heard.

Once more, Jesus is the model of how we should be in our caring. He magnetised the poor and needy, amazed people by his teaching, healing and very presence, and shone with authenticity and integrity. Yet at times, those around him found him puzzling, mysterious and hard to understand. There was a sensitivity and sense of timing in the degree to which he would reveal himself, or allow others to talk of him. In fact, his understanding of the complexity and unreliability of others would lead on occasions to his cautious withdrawal, even in the face of apparent response:

Now while he was in Jerusalem at the Passover Feast, many people saw the miraculous signs he was doing and believed in his name. But Jesus would not entrust himself to them, for he knew all men. He did not need man's testimony about man, for he knew what was in a man. (John 2:23–25)

We see here that Jesus had the measure of human nature and, where he sensed the shallowness or suggestibility of people's response to him, he could withhold his trust in them. Carers and counsellors also need this wisdom for gauging the right level of transparency in their encounters with others. The correct degree of openness or guardedness, coming out of an inner security, is a mark of how free we are to 'be ourselves' in our counselling. Strengthened by a God-given caution, we can be at ease with our clients, liberated from anxiety about status and the impression we are giving, offering our entire, genuine attention.

Non-Possessive Warmth

In all human relating there is the need for personal warmth towards others. Without some measure of kindred feelings, of a sense of a common humanity, most friendships or family ties would soon become sterile and fruitless. And this is also the case in counselling, for where the counsellor despises or rejects the client there is little or no hope of progress. Once more, however, a balance is required because counselling, while needing the seed-bed of human affection, must also have its boundaries well laid out if it is to avoid emotional entanglement with those in need. This *non-possessive warmth* (or 'unconditional positive regard', to use Carl Rogers' phrase) has been defined by Carole Sutton as follows:

Non-possessive warmth [is] an attitude of active and positive caring by the counsellor, conveyed to the client both verbally and non-verbally, but which is directed towards encouraging independence rather than dependency.[6]

We can further understand non-possessive warmth by looking at its constituent qualities of respect and being non-judgmental.

Respect

Many of us respect others for their experience, abilities and skills. In A. A. Milne's *The House at Pooh Corner*, Rabbit reflects to himself about Christopher Robin and says, 'He respects Owl, because you can't help respecting anybody who can spell TUESDAY, even if he doesn't spell it right'.[7] But the counsellor is called primarily to respect the *person* of the one counselled, rather than his or her expertise – even at spelling! The Latin root of the word 'respect' means to look at or regard, and the implication for counselling is that the client is viewed in such a way as to be valued. As Gerard Egan puts it, respect means 'prizing others simply because they are human beings'.[8]

However, just as genuineness needs to be expressed in order to be effective, respect must be *shown* if it is to help the client. If, as a counsellor, I say to a client 'I respect you', and then proceed to gaze out of the window as he pours out his story, twiddling my thumbs and yawning periodically, the client will soon know he has been deceived, and his story will dry up. True respect may occasionally be declared through words, but its most powerful message is shown non-verbally – through adequate eye-contact, an attentive and alert posture, and appropriate gestures and facial expressions. This non-verbal communication, where the counsellor is genuine, will mediate the more hidden aspects of respect, such as taking the person seriously, seeing him or her as unique and special, and being willing to work with the client for his or her growth in maturity. Egan describes respect as 'being "for" the client'; he writes:

This [being 'for' the client] is not a tender or sentimental attitude. The helper is a caring person in a down-to-earth, nonsentimental sense. As a sign of this, respect ultimately involves placing demands on clients or helping them place demands on themselves. This being for, then, refers to clients' basic humanity and to their potential to be more than they are right now. Respect is both gracious and tough-minded.[9]

It is indisputable that Jesus Christ respected everyone who came his way. He knew they had been made in God's image and were fallen and flawed, but also that they were redeemable in relation to him. There is no doubt, too, that his regard for them was clearly shown by word, story, gesture and action, for both sexes and all ages were drawn by the magnet of his love. This valuing of others was never a soft option in which Jesus exuded a cocoon of general good-will to make comfortable all and sundry. His respect for others was, to use Egan's phrase, 'both gracious and tough-minded': he valued people enough to challenge, confront and rebuke, as well as encourage, console and affirm.

The demonstration of this 'tough love' is never easy in counselling as true respect for clients requires a middle course to be steered between colluding with them and rejecting them. In the former, the counsellor, for fear of hurting the person in need, fails to challenge or question the client's dubious attitudes and behaviour. In time, both parties can be locked into an unhealthy relationship, where the counsellor has let the initiative slip and the client has become heavily dependent. In the latter course, where the counsellor confronts far too readily, the client can feel misunderstood and may give up seeking help. In each instance, respect has been lost on both sides.

Where the counsellor's attitude is gracious and tough-minded at the same time, then, as we saw with the prophetic dimension of counselling (see pp. 80–81), any challenging of the client's life will be carried out lovingly. This means that confrontation, if needed, only comes after careful listening and within the relationship of trust. This view holds that it is better for the client to see the error of his or her ways through inner conviction ('I can see at last that I've been irresponsible and foolish . . . I must make amends') rather than through outside intervention. Where the counsellor feels the need to challenge, it is wise to be tentative, since conclusions drawn may be wide of the mark. Confronting sentences which begin with 'Could it be that . . .', 'I wonder if . . .' or 'It seems to me that . . .' are more likely to bear fruit than bald accusation. It is in this way that a true respect for the individual can be held, even where unpleasant realities have to be faced.

Being Non-Judgmental

Many Christians who are new to counselling, especially if they have very clear-cut views on what is right and wrong, find themselves condemning those they seek to help. They may assure themselves that they 'hate the sin, and not the sinner' but, not too far into the counselling process, a deep antipathy may grow up towards the client who seems to resist the counsellor's well-intentioned calls to repentance. There are two opposing mistakes in this area: one is to jump to conclusions, the other is to avoid conclusions.

Jumping to conclusions is the heart of being judgmental. Here, the counsellor is shockable and is taken aback by the inexpressible words or outrageous behaviour of the client. With a little more experience (and after finding, perhaps, that clients tend not to return!) such a counsellor may work hard at concealing his or her displeasure, only to give the game away with a tell-tale narrowing of the eyes or pulling down of the corner of the mouth. The client is not deceived, knows that offence has been given and will adjust by either softening the harsh realities of the story to protect the counsellor, or decide to exaggerate events to expose and enjoy the helper's shockability! Either way, mutual respect is lost – if it was ever found.

The contrary mistake is to suspend all judgment indefinitely. In this situation, the counsellor never quite draws a conclusion, always reasoning that there must be yet another untapped, extenuating circumstance behind the client's wayward life. This endlessly uncritical view can ensnare the counsellor and client into either a collusive relationship of dependency ('My counsellor's such a dear! She's *so* understanding that I *must* go on seeing her') or the trap of manipulation ('My counsellor's so blinkered about what I'm really like that I'll lead him a rare song and dance!').

These examples are, of course, extremes and one of the key aspects of training in counselling – that of encouraging self-awareness – is aimed to keep the trainee from such pitfalls. It is salutary that the context of Jesus' well-known warning, 'Do not judge, or you too will be judged' (Matt. 7:1), is that of humbling self-knowledge. He asks, 'Why do you look at the speck of sawdust in your brother's eye and pay no attention to the plank in your own eye?' (v. 3). Martyn Lloyd-Jones has pointed out that this scene is even worse than the blind leading the blind: it is like having eye surgery from a blind ophthalmologist![10] No, the effective counsellor will be aware of personal 'blind spots' and, with God's help, will deal with those prejudices, conflicts and sins that mar insight and lead to judgmentalism.

But that will not be the end of the matter, for the Christian who cares is still called – once the blight of his or her own failure is exposed and treated – to heed Jesus' words 'to remove the speck from your brother's eye' (v. 5). Being non-judgmental should never stop short of this responsibility. True respect for another realises that both parties are on the same journey – that of seeking the removal of those things that block the path towards maturity. Paul, in the context of the Holy Spirit's work, urges the spiritually mature to take very seriously this call to respect one another:

> Brothers [and sisters], if someone is caught in a sin, you who are spiritual should restore him gently. But watch yourself, or you also may be tempted. Carry each other's burdens, and in this way you will fulfil the law of Christ. (Gal. 6:1–2)

Accurate Empathy

A story is told of a railway passenger who, irritatedly, asked the train driver, 'Can't you go any faster?'. The reply did nothing to lessen his irritation: 'Of course I can! But I've got to stay with the train'. It is this 'staying with' the train that demonstrated the driver's 'empathy' with the vehicle: he was committed to close attention to the controls and signals, and needed to stay in harmony with the train's motion and momentum. We can say that he had an accurate understanding of his train on a moment by moment basis, and this understanding entailed both careful listening and close identification. In the context of counselling, Truax and Carkhuff wrote that with empathy 'we begin to perceive the events and experiences of [another's] life "as if" they were parts of our own life'.[11] Let us look at this 'as if' quality of accurate empathy through the twin perspectives of listening and identification.

Listening

Do you remember the last time you were *really* listened to? At last here was someone who seemed to value you enough to give you time and close attention; everything you said – even the outrageous things – was taken seriously and weighed up thoughtfully; there was no jumping to conclusions, no dismissive asides and no harsh judgments; and, best of all, you *knew* the other person was listening. Such an experience made you feel good: you felt respected, understood, uncondemned and encouraged. Witness a very different situation where two strangers meet, perhaps at a party, a pub or other social gathering, and there is some attempt to get to know each other:

'Hi! My name's Jack. Have I seen you here before?'

'No, this is my first visit. I'm Pete – just moved into the area, you know.'

'How come?'

'Well, it's a long story, Jack. Briefly, my marriage broke up some time ago, the divorce has just come through and so – it was a very difficult decision – I decided to make a move and start again from scratch. Here I am, then, looking for a job. I've been in office work – insurance, you know – but I'd like to try my hand in carpentry or something similar. Always been a bit of a cabinet-maker on the quiet, you know.'

Jack, who has been gazing over Pete's shoulder at another group of people, looks at his watch and says, 'Goodness, is that the time? Must be going. It's been really good chatting, Paul. All the best in the office on Monday. Give my regards to your missus and the family. See you!'

Pete, eager for some understanding and human warmth, feels rebuffed and devalued. He has not been listened to and the likelihood of developing a friendship with Jack is remote.

Learning to listen is a prerequisite for all caring relationships. However, effective listening needs to have two components: a *mental* element which observes, takes note and remembers; and a *social* element which responds appropriately to what is heard. Where someone is content merely to record mentally the details of what is being said or done we can talk of 'passive' listening; where there is a clear demonstration of attendance to those details, we refer to 'active' listening. In everyday life, a mother who hears her baby crying in distress but prefers to watch to the end of her favourite television programme before assessing the situation, cannot be said to be a model of listening! Neither is the husband who carries on reading the evening paper while his wife recounts the ups and downs of her day, even though he insists he has heard every word! It is *active* listening that reassures the one listened to.

Rarely are the mental and social aspects of listening more required than in counselling, where people in need come, perhaps half-heartedly, to share their stories in order to find solutions to their problems. Once more, we see that the counsellor must not only pick up the facts of the narrative (this person's name is Liz, she is twenty-eight, unmarried, is the eldest of three, her father died of a heart attack last year, she is out of work, feels desperately unhappy, etc.) but must *show* that the story line is followed and understood – and this is done largely through non-verbal means. Adequate eye-contact, an attentive posture, appropriate facial expression and an occasional word to encourage continuation are more effective than, say, a repeated declaration, against the evidence, that we really are listening!

The importance of faithful attending comes through in a story about Frieda Fromm-Reichmann, a psychoanalyst who fled the Nazi regime to settle in the United States. Soon after her arrival, and before she had had time to adjust to a new culture, she was consulted by a wealthy American man. Some years later, it is said while fund-raising, she received a generous donation from her former patient who acclaimed how helpful she had been. She admitted to him that at the time of the consultation she had hardly understood a word of English. She had evidently shown the qualities of a good active listener, encouraging the unravelling of his barely comprehended tale by her nods and encouraging grunts![12]

The principle of listening is clearly laid down in the Bible. God himself is one who listens and responds: to Adam's need for a companion (Gen. 2:18); to the man and the woman in their shame (Gen. 3:9–13); to Abel's blood crying out against his brother (Gen. 4:10); to Hezekiah's prayer for healing (2 Kgs 20:5); to the basic needs of his creation (Job 38:41); to the psalmist's 'cry for mercy' (Ps. 28:2,6); and, supremely, to his praying, obedient Son (Mark 14:35–36; John 17; Heb. 5:7).

The listening God is our example. We, too, are to be good listeners: to him and to one another. We are to hear him in and through his creation: in the sighing of the wind, the crash of the waves and the rumble of thunder, in a natural order whose 'voice goes out into all the earth' (Ps. 19:4). We are to hear him in and through his declared word: a word that nourishes and sustains (Deut. 8:3; Ps. 19:10), brings wisdom (Ps. 19:7; Prov. 1:5), warns (Ps. 19:11), exposes (Heb. 4:12–13) and protects (Eph. 6:17). Our greatest attention, though, is to be focused on Christ himself, the Word made flesh. As we read in the account of his transfiguration:

> Then a cloud appeared and enveloped them, and a voice came
> from the cloud: 'This is my Son, whom I love. Listen to him!'.
> (Mark 9:7)

Just as God himself both listens and responds, we too, in
listening to Christ, are called to a response. As Jesus said to
the woman in the crowd: 'Blessed . . . are those who hear the
word of God and obey it' (Luke 11:28). The Bible is clear that our
listening is not to be passive but active. This applies both to our
relating to God and to one another. James shows the essential
link between listening and action – negatively, as in containing
rash speech and wrongful anger:

> Everyone should be quick to listen, slow to speak and slow
> to become angry, for man's anger does not bring about the
> righteous life that God desires. (Jas 1:19–20)

And positively, in hearing what God calls us to and then living
out his ways in practical obedience: 'Do not merely listen to the
word, and so deceive yourselves. Do what it says' (Jas 1:22).

And so, counselling, spiritual direction and the healing ministries are at their best when the carer is an attentive and
responsive listener. People who seek help need to be heard.
As we have seen, this requires that the one who cares not
only gets the facts right but demonstrates understanding. The
story is everything: those in need long to tell their tale, share
the ups and downs of life and find relief for their anguish. It is
the good listener, who listens in the quiet places to God and
then mediates his compassion and God-given wisdom, who brings
solace. The Book of Isaiah points to God's obedient servant,
who says:

> The Sovereign Lord has given me an instructed tongue, to
> know the word that sustains the weary. He wakens me
> morning by morning, wakens my ear to listen like one being
> taught. (Isa. 50:4)

Identification

Although listening gives the carer a bridgehead in helping others, it is 'identification' that is most likely to bridge the gap of communication between two people. The ability to identify with another and express that sense of solidarity is underlined by Truax and Carkhuff when they write:

> At a *high* level of accurate empathy the message 'I am *with* you' is unmistakably clear – the therapist's remarks fit perfectly with the client's mood and content.[13]

It is the ability to gauge mood, as well as content, accurately that is so vital to giving the message 'I am with you'. And in order to assess the complexities of other people's emotions, the counsellor needs, as we have already seen, a considerable degree of self-awareness and inner harmony, as well as attitudes that are non-judgmental and respectful of the client. If the helper is out of touch with his or her own feelings, is riven with inner conflict, driven by mixed motives or lacking in compassion towards the client, then the chances of successful bridge-building are remote. The counsellor is not free enough within to reach out, and the client feels too threatened or puzzled by the would-be helper to respond.

In the early stages of counselling someone, the prime need is to attend to the details of the story as presented; this accurate understanding can be called *basic* empathy. In time, if there is to be substantial help offered, *advanced* empathy must come into play. Here, it is often necessary to dig deeper, to read between the lines of what is said, to note where non-verbal communication does not tie up with the story line and to probe further into the emotional content of the client's life.

Although it may seem a far cry from the counselling room to the stable at Bethlehem, some have drawn an analogy between the incarnation and the identification needed in accurate empathy. Thomas Oden, in particular, has discussed this correlation, writing:

[In the incarnation], God assumes our frame of reference, entering into our human situation of finitude and estrangement, sharing our human condition even unto death.[14]

Clearly, we see in the self-emptying of Christ, 'being made in human likeness' (Phil. 2:7), complete identification with the limitations and suffering of our humanity. Here was one who entered 'our frame of reference', knowing hunger and thirst, feeling our pains and sorrows and sharing our joys and celebrations. In this taking on of our finiteness, he 'became obedient to death – even death on a cross' (Phil. 2:8) and herein is the ultimate identification: for 'God made him who had no sin to be sin for us, so that in him we might become the righteousness of God' (2 Cor. 5:21). Whatever our understanding of this mystery, we can say that he became like us, that we might become like him.

This wondrous perspective – of a God who cares enough to be with us, even in the darkest place – is for all time and for all situations, not least that of counselling, where the darkness often surfaces. We, too, in the name of Christ and in the power of the Spirit, are called to enter into the lives of others, learning to 'rejoice with those who rejoice' and 'mourn with those who mourn' (Rom. 12:15). At times this venture will feel a lonely one but, even in the bleakest places of human need, we are assured of the presence of God, who can identify with and reach the most bereft. This is the God who, in the words of Donald Capps, seems to say to those who are so shattered by life's onslaughts that they cannot lift their heads: 'If I were in your shoes, and you in mine, I would have difficulty praising you'.[15]

Questions for Discussion

1. List the qualities you would most like to see in someone you might seek help from. Discuss why you value these qualities.
2. Compare this list of qualities with those described in this chapter: congruence, transparency, respect, non-judgmentalism, the ability to listen, and identification. Try to find useful synonyms for these words.

3. Galatians 5:22–23 declares that 'the fruit of the Spirit is love, joy, peace, patience, kindness, goodness, faithfulness, gentleness and self-control'. We can see these virtues as descriptive of Christ and a picture of growing Christlikeness in the believer. Discuss how these qualities relate, if at all, to those of genuineness, non-possessive warmth and accurate empathy.

Personal Reflection

Sandor Ferenczi, the Hungarian psychoanalyst, said that the 'indispensable healing power in the therapeutic gift is love'.[16] We find, too, that love heads up the list of qualities named within the fruit of the Spirit (Gal. 5:22–23). To bear this fruit is to be Christlike and it is in him that we find the love of God perfected. The healing power of Jesus Christ, as he reached out to people in need, is his love – for God, his neighbour, his friends, his enemies.

Read 1 Corinthians 13 slowly and reflectively, asking God to show you the quality of love in Jesus Christ. After reading the passage two or three times, put the name 'Jesus' where the word 'love' occurs in verses four to seven:

> Jesus is patient, he is kind. He does not envy, does not boast, is not proud. He is not rude, is not self-seeking, is not easily angered, keeps no record of wrongs. Jesus does not delight in evil but rejoices with the truth. He always protects, always trusts, always hopes, always perseveres.

These statements point to many aspects of the fruit of the Spirit. Read these in Galatians 5:22–23. Choose one or two and try to picture Jesus demonstrating his love through patience, kindness, gentleness or self-control, etc. A choice of any of these Gospel passages may help you: Matthew 9:18–26; 12:9–14; 14:22–36; 15:21–28; Mark 7:31–37; 10:17–22; 14:32–42; 53–65; Luke 7:36–50; 13:31–35; John 8:1–11; 11:17–44; 16:17–33; 21:15–23.

Return to 1 Corinthians 13 and reread verses one to three.

Think about your own life and your activities. Make a list of the main things you do and write them out in the following form; for example:

If I spend all my time feeding, clothing and occupying the children, but have not love, I am nothing. If I work hard in the office all day, but have not love, I gain nothing. If I spend many hours caring and counselling, but have not love, I am nothing . . .

Finally, return to verses four to seven and ask the Lord to enrich you with his love in all your relating, caring, counselling and bringing of healing to others. You may like to use this prayer:

Lord Christ, I thank you for your love so strong
May that love flow through me to others
May I be patient when change comes slowly
May I be kind when life seems harsh
May I be gentle when others feel bruised
May I be humble when things go well
May I be peaceful when anger rises within
May I forgive when wronged
May I rejoice when the truth is discovered
Love never fails, but I do
May I hope when things seem hopeless
May I persevere when the way is hard.

7

Long-term Aims: Changing the Future

We must learn a love that makes others mature instead of
smothering them or glorifying them.
                                    Elisabeth Moltmann-Wendel

One of the hardest things in life is to look ahead with any degree
of confidence. In 1979, after eight months' blindness and the
restoration of vision to my right eye (see p. 73), I keenly
anticipated starting a new medical job as a clinical assistant in
a psychiatric hospital. The consultant who wanted me to work
with him had already waited many months for the recovery of my
sight and so, with my improved health, we agreed that I would
start the job that autumn. However, this was not to be, for,
just one month before taking up the appointment, I went blind
for the second time and this reality, coupled with the malaise I
was experiencing from brucellosis, meant that the post had to
go to someone else.

Someone has said, 'Prediction is not difficult so long as one
steers clear of the future'. As needy individuals seek care
and counsel, how are those who offer help able to encourage
them as they face troubled futures? We have, surely, to accept
the unpredictability of what lies ahead but, at the same time,
see that, under God, the future can be fashioned favourably
by decisions and adjustments made now. In this context we
must ask, What are the aims of counselling? In chapter four,

we defined counselling in terms of its quest for 'constructive change' in people's lives. What exactly is this constructive change and what are the markers along the way which show that change is being effected? Let us look at these questions as we consider long-term *aims* in this chapter and intermediate *goals* in chapter eight.

The aims of counselling and psychotherapy have been variously expressed: Jung's analytical psychology talks of 'individuation'; humanistic approaches seek 'self-actualisation'; transactional analysis (TA) works towards human 'autonomy'; Gestalt therapy aims at 'unitary functioning'; and transpersonal methods pursue, variously, 'psychosynthesis', 'no-boundary awareness' and 'cosmic consciousness'. As a generalisation, it can be said that these aims, and others like them, show a range of ideas about the integration of the self, both within the person and in relation to the world around. Historically, and increasingly towards the end of the twentieth century, Western therapies have leant Eastwards. As a result, the quest for a sense of self has given way to a search for release from self-consciousness and everyday duties into the oceanic bliss of reunion with *Brahman*, the Hindu concept of the 'Universal Self', or the state of *Nirvana*, the Buddhist vision of nothingness or self-extinction.[1]

In contrast to the direction taken by many humanistic and transpersonal approaches, counselling that is truly Christian aims to enhance not only a sense of self and of others but also of the Godhead, without entering the trap of self-intrigue on the one hand or dropping into the void of self-annihilation on the other. As we saw in chapter two, the image of God can be restored in our lives through Christ, re-establishing our sense of identity individually, corporately and as part of the created order. In chapter four, we looked further at this notion of increasing Christlikeness as we considered how spiritual direction, counselling and the healing ministries seek to encourage us all towards maturity and wholeness. We can say, from our study of humanity – created, fallen and redeemed – that the ultimate aim of all Christian caring must be maturity in Christ.

Stephen Pattison brings out this emphasis of completeness, adulthood and wholeness in his discussion on the nature of pastoral care:

> Pastoral care is that activity, undertaken especially by representative Christian persons, directed towards the elimination of sin and sorrow and the presentation of all people perfect in Christ to God.[2]

Let us consider two main hallmarks of the maturity we seek: *integration* and *love*.

Integration

It has been traditional to split a consideration of constructive change in people's lives into psychological and spiritual maturity. However, as we have seen, we have been created living unities and so we should not be surprised to find that growth in Christian maturity involves both psychological and spiritual factors. David Benner makes the point strongly:

> The spiritual quest is, at one level, a psychological quest, and every psychological quest in some way reflects the basic spiritual quest. Furthermore, psychological and spiritual aspects of human functioning are inextricably connected, and any segregation of spirituality and psychology is, therefore, both artificial and destructive.[3]

The links between mental stress and bodily symptoms are well known and we talk readily of the way certain skin conditions, some forms of asthma, instances of high blood pressure and a variety of stomach and gut problems are tied into negative thinking and anxious attitudes. We can see the connections between such psychosomatic states and views which declare, respectively, that we cannot bear others to touch us, that their presence is stifling, that they make our blood boil, cause us to feel sick or turn us inside out.

By the same token, we need to see the intimate interweaving of the psychological and the spiritual. Alison, in her mid-twenties and working as a librarian, had, along with her two brothers, a very possessive mother who had always sought to live the lives of her offspring for them. As a result, Alison found the whole process of growing up and moving away from her parents' home extremely difficult. A loner by nature, her few childhood friends had always been carefully vetted by her mother and, during her teen years, boys seemed to pose a continual threat to the family's solidarity. Going on holiday, leaving home for college and moving into a flat in a nearby city all proved very upsetting as she faced separation from her mother. Although from a Baptist background, it was while studying librarianship that, through another young woman who had befriended her, Alison consciously committed herself to Christ. Although it gave her a new sense of direction, her faith was continually assailed by feelings of panic over relationships and the recurring anguish she experienced while away from her mother.

Over a protracted period of counselling, Alison gradually developed a basic trust in her counsellor and a somewhat precarious confidence in her first boy-friend, a young teacher who attended the same local church. Step by step, her fears and anxieties were faced, understood, prayed over and exposed to biblical perspectives of trust and obedience. Her increasing sense of Christ's presence and power has given her many small victories in her relating to others – not least towards her mother, about whom she became able to think and talk more objectively and in more adult ways. At such times, she came across to the counsellor as 'authentic Alison' rather than as a pitiable young woman who longed to return to an infantile dependency.

In Alison, delayed psychological adjustment and a new spiritual dimension went hand in hand to bring her a measure of progress towards maturity. Although her openness to God was fundamental in shaping her future, it was only as she learned to face up to her psychological insecurity and move out in tentative trust towards others that the Spirit's transforming work could be effected. Benner's observation, 'Until one *has* a self it is difficult to *transcend* self',[4] seems particularly applicable to Alison's story.

It is undeniable that psychological and spiritual factors work in harness to establish maturity, but we should not argue that it is only the psychologically sound who can scale the spiritual heights. Here, I am reminded of Jonathan, a slow learner who is considerably handicapped by a birth injury. His lack of social sophistication and psychological finesse is wonderfully offset by his loving nature and godly wisdom. Learned and lengthy theological discussion has to look over its shoulder when Jonathan is present for, listening silently for the most part, he can cap a half-hour interchange on, say, the 'complexity of personal response to the deity of Christ' with a devastating summary: 'So, we are to love Jesus?'

Conversely, we should also avoid the mistaken view that spiritual vitality is inevitably accompanied by psychological integration. There are many Christian leaders in the public eye, for example, who can preach powerfully and evangelise effectively, and yet whose social skills and psychological adjustment leave a great deal to be desired. This disparity should not alarm us unduly for God is able to empower whom he will; but, at the same time, where the Holy Spirit is at work and there is human response, greater stability and maturity will follow. Benner helpfully summarises the integrating effects of growth in psychological and spiritual maturity in these words:

Psychospiritual maturity is characterised by integration of personality, which occurs within a context of significant interpersonal relationships and surrender to God. In this surrender we discover our true selves. The integrated self, which is the endpoint of this process, is both an achievement and a gift. In deepening intimate union with God we find the selves he gives us; we become the selves we were intended to be from eternity.[5]

Love

Just as psychological and spiritual maturity join together and are expressed in the integration of the personality, so social and relational maturity fuse in the expression of love – love of God, neighbour and oneself. We have already seen, in chapter three, how Christian love is the mainspring of all true pastoral care. One of the cardinal aims of caring and counselling is to engender that same love in the attitudes and actions of those who seek growth in maturity.

Love of God

Perhaps one of the hardest things for any of us to know is how much, or how little, we really love God. Jesus, echoing the Old Testament, declared this to be the 'first and greatest commandment' (Matt. 22:38). We are, put so simply and yet so profoundly, to love the Lord our God with all our 'heart', 'soul' and 'mind': with every fibre of our being – thinking, feeling, imagining, assessing, doing, relating, praising, wondering . . . This is our calling, to respond with love to the One who is the source of love and of all loving. Inevitably, in our struggle to return the divine love, we falter and fall short. As Leanne Payne puts it, quoting Augustine's prayer, 'Set love in order in me': 'We love confusedly, we fallen ones; the journey of life is for setting love in order'.[6]

As carers and counsellors, it is only when we allow the God of love to forgive us, purify our motives and raise us up again and again that we can encourage those we try to help in this 'journey of life for setting love in order'. Fortunately, we are not left to flounder, for it is the tide of his love that overwhelms and stirs us into loving. For me, as for countless others, it has been a fresh appreciation of the sufferings of Christ that has nudged me into that response.

Following the Hebridean holiday, described in chapter four (see pp. 73–74), and the renewed onset of my blindness, Joy and I returned home to face the uncertain future. Now blind *and* debilitated by brucellosis, obliged to retire from my work as a medical officer in Student Health and also needing to relinquish the promised post in psychiatry, the outlook was bleak. After a month or two, however, there arose the prospect of a second major operation on my right eye with the possibility, once more, of restored vision. Although profoundly frustrated by recurring blindness and one-eyed sightedness, and longing to settle for one or the other, it seemed right to face surgery again. It was on coming round from the anaesthetic on the open ward that I had a fresh experience of the suffering love of Christ. Not long after the event, I described it with these words:

While my consciousness came and went, I realised that I was lying flat, that my right eye was bandaged and the operation was over. While I lay there I began to feel waves of nausea and panic. I should not, and indeed could not, move my head and yet I had an overwhelming need to sit up. I longed to rise and take deep breaths of life-saving air . . . the sense of isolation and helpless prostration continued to torment. I wanted to cry out but could not.

I tried to pray and evoke an awareness of the Lord's presence. He was, of course, there all the time, watching me. I had a sense, in my own anguish, of His infinitely greater suffering . . . Through it all, the agony of Golgotha seemed to supersede and engulf my own moderate sufferings . . . I saw, while I wondered, that at least the busy nurses were on my side – they comforted, reassured, gave sips of water – but this Man had been completely bereft and rejected. I suffered a little, surrounded by care – He had suffered inestimably, surrounded by a cursing crowd. In my brief span of helplessness, I took great comfort from His all-helping helplessness. He had overcome the darkness of the abyss. His victory encompassed all.[7]

It was through these renewed insights into the suffering Christ that Joy and I took comfort amidst our continuing uncertainties. We could and would survive: loved, we too would learn new levels of loving. In more recent years, the writing of Julian of Norwich has been one of the influences that has helped encapsulate for me the awesome simplicity of being loved and loving in return:

> Our Lord God means in as many words, 'Look! Here you have material for humility, for love, for total self-denial, for enjoying me. Because I love you, enjoy me! This will please me most of all'.[8]

Love of Others

Tales of loving others that catch the imagination are rare. They tend, by definition, to be set in times of crisis and hardship. One rightly well-known story is that of Father Maximillian Kolbe, a Roman Catholic priest held with six hundred men on one of the cell blocks in the infamous concentration camp of Auschwitz, during World War II. One summer's day in 1941 a prisoner escaped from a work party and, following an unsuccessful search, the camp commander declared that ten men would be chosen at random and shot if the escapee was not found within twenty-four hours. The prisoner was not found, the ten were selected and assembled for their death. At the last minute, Father Maximillian, knowing the personal circumstances of one of the detainees – Gajowniczek, a Polish soldier with a family – volunteered to take his place. Thirty years later, the Pope, recalling the horrors of Nazi imperialism, said this:

> Millions of beings were sacrificed to the pride of force and the madness of racialism. But in the darkness there glows the figure of Maximillian Kolbe. Over that immense antechamber of death there hovers his divine and imperishable word of life: redeeming love.[9]

Such self-sacrificing love is rare, and is a clear indication that God is loved too. Jesus made the connection explicit when he completed his declaration that we are to love God with all our being, as the 'first and greatest commandment', with the statement that 'the second is like it: "Love your neighbour as yourself"' (Matt. 22:39). John sees Christ's Calvary love as the mainspring of self-giving:

> This is how we know what love is: Jesus Christ laid down his life for us. And we ought to lay down our lives for our brothers. If anyone has material possessions and sees his brother in need but has no pity on him, how can the love of God be in him? (1 John 3:16–17)

As John indicates, our call is not exclusively to the supreme sacrifice, although none of us knows whether we might one day face a challenge to our loving of the order of Father Kolbe's heroism. The challenge is to achieve a level of caring that is essentially practical: it is about perceiving the needs of others and meeting those needs without fuss or fanfare. And, ultimately, as we have seen, the greatest need we all have is for fulfilment, for wholeness and maturity. As we learn to exercise a neighbourly love which responds to specific needs, so we can encourage others towards mature loving. This caring enterprise will be neither possessive nor idealising. As Elisabeth Moltmann-Wendel puts it:

> We have to relearn what loving means; we must learn a love that makes others mature instead of smothering them or glorifying them, a love that creates an area in which there is no domination.[10]

Love of Oneself

The levitical commandment, 'Love your neighbour as yourself', is given a powerful imprimatur throughout the New Testament. Sanctioned by Jesus himself,[11] both Paul and James stress the supremacy of this summary of the entire law[12]: it is the 'one rule' whereby 'love is the fulfilment of the law' (Rom. 13:9–10); it is 'the perfect law that gives freedom' (Jas 1:25); and it is 'the royal law' of Scripture which, if kept, shows true righteousness (Jas 2:8).

Undoubtedly, the thrust of the command is that we should love others: indeed, *all* others, as Jesus clearly demonstrates when he urges us to love those least desirable neighbours – our enemies! In fact, this all-embracing love is as clear a marker as any that we are partaking of Christian maturity and completeness, for Jesus puts the command: 'Love your enemies' in the context of the ultimate injunction: 'Be perfect (*teleios*), therefore, as your heavenly Father is perfect' (Matt. 5:43–48).

And yet the command is, 'Love your neighbour as yourselves', and not simply 'Love your neighbour', or 'Love your neighbour instead of yourselves'. We can, of course, make too much of the phrase 'as yourselves' and see it, wrongly, as a bid for self-indulgence. In fact, such an interpretation is inconsistent, for just as our call to love our neighbour is an invitation to meet his or her truest needs, so, by inference, our care for ourselves will be a commitment to our highest good. The biblical implication, true as ever to the realities of human nature, seems to be that we can only love others effectively and reliably if we already have an appropriate self-regard. As Augustine of Hippo said to his congregation: 'I won't tell you how to love your neighbour as I am not sure whether you have as yet learned to love yourselves'.[13]

There is no doubt that one of the cardinal features of distorted living which leads people to seek counselling is that of inadequate self-regard. This may have its roots in a range of childhood insecurities, from downright rejection (this child of ours is not bright enough, beautiful enough, is not the right sex, is one too many, is nothing more than an intrusion . . .) to the opposite extreme of excessive spoiling (this child of ours is brighter, more beautiful than others, is the one and only, is all we live for . . .). In the first instance, the emerging adolescent and young adult is likely to nurse a deep sense of unworthiness (I am unlovable: since others do not love me, I cannot love myself). In the second, the person may grow up with an inflated view of self (I am excessively lovable: how can others survive without me?) that does not match the negative reactions of others; as this false self hears the uneasy whisperings of the true self, low self-esteem may set in (In spite of everything, I'm only a sham; behind all the bluster, I do not like what I see). David Benner explains that, at its best, psychotherapy (and, I would add, counselling) makes us aware of how the false self blocks the way to true self-fulfilment. He adds:

> We are then able to respond to the inner spiritual call, to crucify self-centeredness, and to look to God rather than self as the Lord of our lives. Crucifying the idolatrous self-as-god, we are then free to know ourselves as we never could before; we can now know and actualise our self-in-God.[14]

It is the Holy Spirit, often working through the care and counsel of others, who can break into the vicious circle of low self-esteem, fear of further rejection by others and a lack of trust in a God who seems distant and judgmental. Slowly and falteringly, step by step, those who were apparently trapped can experience the divine reversal, whereby God's love in Christ can begin to warm cold and lonely hearts into life. Loved by the Beloved they learn that, after all, they are lovable, and small stirrings of responsive love begin – towards the impoverished self, towards neglected others and towards a once estranged God.

Questions for Discussion

1. Discuss what you mean by terms like 'psychological maturity' and 'spiritual maturity'. Are they essentially the same thing? Do they pull in the same direction? Do they work against each other? You may like to refer back to Colossians 1:28–29 and

Ephesians 4:11–16 (see question four at the end of chapter four).

2. Discuss any time in your own lives (perhaps in a period of transition, such as adolescence or mid-life, during an illness or bereavement, or at a time of momentous decision) when psychological and spiritual factors have played their part. Does the outcome of your discussion tend to agree with David Benner when he wrote, 'psychological and spiritual aspects of human functioning are inextricably connected' (see p. 113)?

3. Discuss the relationship between Jesus' summary of the Law in Matthew 22:37–40 and the aims of pastoral care and counselling, as described in this chapter. Try to keep in mind the response to Jesus' words of both the carer and those cared for. For example, what might the command, 'Love your neighbour as yourself', mean for a client who struggles with self-centredness or for a counsellor who finds it hard to like his or her client?

4. Look once more at the quotation which heads this chapter (see also p. 119) in order to consider the love 'that makes others mature'. Consider examples (from your own and others' experience) where there has been a 'smothering' or 'glorifying' of others rather than a true loving. Discuss practical steps for creating 'an area in which there is no domination' in your caring and counselling.

5. Low self-esteem is probably the commonest single factor behind requests for counselling. Why do you think this is? Discuss some of the reasons for poor self-regard. How is it that God's love, often mediated through others, can begin to encourage an appropriate self-affirmation? See, for example: Psalm 139:1–18; John 8:1–11; 1 John 4:9–12, 19.

Personal Reflection

Some find the idea of a 'faith biography' helpful, where God's dealings with us in the past are recollected, written down and thought through. Write out the milestones in your own story but pay particular attention to those times of awareness of God's loving and caring towards you. You might call this exercise a 'love biography'. Also record something of your experience of the love of others and of your own love reaching out. Include, where you can, times when you have found some progress in your own regard for yourself, in your specialness, giftedness and essential being. Spend some time looking back through your story and thank God afresh for every insight of his love, of the love of others, and of your own love for other people and yourself. Recall the biblical perspective as recorded in 1 John 4:19: 'We love because he first loved us'.

(Some of you may find this exercise difficult, feeling that you have never experienced love – whether from your parents, from other family members or from anyone else, let alone from God. Give yourself time with the 'biography', nonetheless, asking God to show you evidence of his love, however modest.)

As you look back, you are bound to see something of your own lack of love towards God, others and yourself. You may find, for example, that many of your efforts to care for others have turned sour, spoilt by surprising levels of possessiveness, competitiveness or vanity within yourself.

Maybe you are seeing for the first time how mixed your motives have been in your relating to and caring for others. Jean Vanier has written this of the breaking down of barriers between people:

> For the dismantled barriers permit the rising
> not only of the waters of new life,
> but also of the forces of darkness,
> our need to possess,
> our desire to hold on to people to fill our emptiness,
> the eruption of jealousy
> and with it the capacity to hate.
> Love is gentle and beautiful
> but there comes with it a terrible fear:
> fear of the future
> and of the risk of getting too involved;
> fear that it will lead only to the death

of our so-called freedom,
fear too of being hurt,
for to love is to become vulnerable;
to love is always a risk.[15]

In the context of a call to service, the apostle Paul wrote:

For God did not give us a spirit of timidity, but a spirit of power, of love and of self-discipline (2 Tim. 1:7).

Ask God's forgiveness for the poverty of your loving and seek his fresh enabling to care and love in the words of this prayer (the collect for the Seventh Sunday after Pentecost from *The Alternative Service Book*):

Lord, you have taught us
that all our doings without love are nothing worth.
Send your Holy Spirit and
pour into our hearts that most excellent gift of love,
the true bond of peace and of all virtues,
without which whoever lives is counted dead before you.
Grant this for the sake of your only Son,
Jesus Christ our Lord.

8

Intermediate Goals: Changing the Present

Have a heart that never hardens, and a temper that never tires, and a touch that never hurts.

Charles Dickens

In order to progress towards the ultimate aim of psychological and spiritual maturity, intermediate goals must be set to give the counselling direction and momentum. This should be a joint enterprise in which the counsellor and client anticipate a series of staging-posts along the way. Realistic goal-setting can only arise as insight is gained and perspectives change. When a client comes to the point where, for example, she can say, 'I now see how unforgiving I've been towards my husband and I long to put things right', or where another can admit, 'I realise how my self-pity has held me in bondage for years and I want now to break out of that prison', the way is opened towards effective goal-setting.

In chapter two, we saw how God gave the man and the woman freedom and responsibility within the garden, and how, through human rebellion, these gifts were distorted into licence and bondage. We can now pick up the twin themes of freedom and responsibility once again, for these are crucial goals on the road to Christian maturity. We need to add the third dimension of reconciliation for, in a fallen world, the experience of responsibility and freedom is often closely linked with reparation and forgiveness.

Responsibility

Responsibility is one of those rather heavy words, like accountability and answerability, that often denote burdens, duty, commitment; it is something that we take on, shoulder, maintain or, given half the chance, give up. Although the word commonly has these leaden connotations, it is rooted in the idea of 'response-ability', the ability to respond to God, to others, to one's inner needs, and to situations.

We can usually recognise and admire the responsibility of maturity. The story of Dr Margaret Spufford, the historian, is a case in point. Suffering herself from frequently incapacitating pain due to osteoporosis, she and her husband shouldered their responsibilities, often against the odds, when their younger child, Bridget, was diagnosed as having cystinosis, a rare, genetically-caused metabolic disease which could well prove fatal between the ages of seven and fourteen. In her exquisitely written book *Celebration*, Dr Spufford traces the family's tragic tale with a mixture of practical straightforwardness and anguished questioning on the mystery of suffering. We see the Spuffords' ability to respond, despite enormous strain, to the daily challenge in this brief extract:

> The stress lay in the nature of the situation itself: nursing a child who would have died without constant and continuous medical interference, knowing with accurate foreknowledge that she was going to die in a few years, and transforming this situation to a 'normal', good, loving, family life that felt as ordinary as possible, given the nursing restrictions. It is an almost impossibly taxing situation.[1]

For such a family, the call to responsible living can continue in an acute form beyond the point when others may begin to relax. Bridget, aided by parental devotion, steady medical care and two kidney transplants, survived into early adult life. Reflecting on this phase, her mother, now in her fifties, wrote:

> Even if the lesson of the last few years has been that you must not and cannot protect your child from living, or from pain either, there is a profound irony. She still needs us available to give her a sense of security and of being continuously loved through these experiences, even though we are now totally powerless. We are, as it were 'invisible' since she is an 'adult'. Yet we are still also completely responsible . . . Now she has failed, inevitably in all this medicine, to keep up with her peer group, to move on from home after her 'A' levels, into further training or a job, she is often alone at home, often unwell, often agonisingly lonely.[2]

The Spuffords' story is simply an example, albeit a poignant one, of the harsh realities and call to responsibility faced by many. In counselling, as in everyday life, the road to increased maturity is through the acceptance of daily responsibility. There are no short-cuts. The unemployed youngster who is depressed may need, as his gloom begins to lift, to be encouraged to face the realities of filling in forms, seeking careers advice and making the most of friendships. The anxious young mother, weighed down by the demands of small children and a largely absent husband, may be helped to look into the possibilities of an available crèche, find some space to develop her own interests and issue a challenge to her husband to play his part. The retired couple, who have grown complacent and bored with each other, may begin to respond to an intermediate goal of greater responsibility where they learn to listen to each other, take appropriate steps to live more healthily and ask themselves what part they can realistically play in the neighbourhood.

With such possibilities in mind, programmes need to be considered to set out ways of achieving the desired goals. It is at this point that specific aims need clarification. And so, to take the example of the young mother, it will be important to help her establish just what interests she wants to cultivate, before she embarks on a detailed plan which might include visits to the local library, writing letters for information on workshops, tracking down a like-minded friend and arranging regular babysitting so she can attend evening classes.

It is within this area of intermediate goals that Christian counsellors are often impatient. Longing to see far-reaching change in the lives of those they try to help, they may fail to realise that such epic transformation comes slowly, if at all. The fruit of Christian maturity, even when set through God's work of grace, may ripen with exceeding slowness. The mistake is to think that you can rush fruit-bearing, forgetting the importance of daily cultivation and a productive environment. The responsibilities of daily decisions and faithful living, albeit nurtured by the love of God and the support of others, are the modest building blocks of long-term growth. Thinking of the countless individuals who struggle to live responsibly against the odds, we can take heart from the example of Christ. Even for him, the path of fulfilment was long and arduous:

> During the days of Jesus' life on earth, he offered up prayers and petitions with loud cries and tears to the one who could save him from death, and he was heard because of his reverent submission. Although he was a son, he learned obedience from what he suffered and, once made perfect (complete, whole, mature), he became the source of eternal salvation for all who obey him . . . (Heb. 5:7–9)

Reconciliation

We all need reconciliation. At first, the man and the woman in Eden did not: as long as they kept responsibly within the bounds of their God-given freedom, the channels of grace and love with each other and with their Creator were open. It was human sin that blocked the flow of fellowship. As we saw in chapter two (pp. 34–35), it is Jesus Christ who comes to bring together, to reconcile fallen humanity and the Lord God. As Paul puts it in a classic New Testament passage:

> Therefore, if anyone is in Christ, he is a new creation; the old has gone, the new has come! All this is from God, who reconciled us to himself through Christ and gave us the ministry of reconciliation: that God was reconciling the world to himself in Christ, not counting men's sins against them. And he has committed to us the message of reconciliation. (2 Cor. 5:17–19)

This reconciliation, this 'at-one-ment', is, in the first place, with God himself and is brought about through the mystery of the sinless dying for the sins of the sinful, in order to restore them to Godlikeness: 'God made him who had no sin to be sin for us, so that in him we might become the righteousness of God' (2 Cor. 5:21). From this glorious re-uniting of Creator and created, we are called to 'the ministry of reconciliation', seeking renewed fellowship with God and, thereby, with one another.

In the context of our objectives in pastoral care and counselling, this ministry of reconciliation can be seen in two parts: *forgiveness* and *friendship*.

Forgiveness

For many of us, one of the most moving examples of forgiveness was seen amongst the survivors of the IRA bomb outrage in Enniskillen in Northern Ireland on Armistice Day, 1987. Gordon Wilson, whose twenty-two-year-old daughter, Marie, was killed, particularly captured the public imagination. A few days after the tragedy, he recalled how, caught up with her amidst the wreckage, he had asked her two or three times, 'Marie, are you all right?' She stoically reassured him, though at times her screams belied her confidence. The last thing she said to him was, 'Dad, I love you very much'; she died, soon after, on the way to hospital. Mr Wilson said this during his interview: 'I've lost a daughter . . . she was such a pet . . . she loved her work as a nurse . . . Yet God is good . . . She's in heaven . . . we'll meet again'. One young Roman Catholic sister recollected comforting victims and their relatives at the local hospital, and added:

> They forgive the way Christ would have forgiven. There was a cloud of darkness over the town that day . . . a cloud of darkness over me. I remember that evening experiencing the light of Christ once again.[3]

It is hard to deny the power of forgiving others who have harmed you or those you love. It is the example of the One who could pray, 'Father, forgive them, for they do not know what they are doing' (Luke 23:34) that makes such largeness of spirit possible. And yet, this is no easy path. Gordon Wilson, interviewed three years after his daughter's murder, found it hard to use the word forgiveness of those terrorists who, tragically, *did* know what they were doing. Even so, God's reconciling love shone through his words: 'I bear no ill-will. I bear no grudge . . . I pray for those guys. I pray that a little of the love of God might come to their hearts and they might receive it'.

The Bible sets great store by the need to forgive one another. In the Old Testament, we see, amongst others, the examples of the reconciliation between Jacob and Esau (Gen. 33:4), Joseph and his brothers (Gen. 50:17), Job and his so-called friends (Job 42:10) and between Hosea and Gomer (Hos. 3:1–3). In the New Testament, a range of principles relating to forgiveness are clarified: it is to be in response to another's desire to make amends (Luke 17:3–4); limitless in its scope (Matt. 18:21–22; Col. 3:13); a mark of Christian love (2 Cor. 2:7–8); a means of outwitting the Enemy (2 Cor. 2:10–11); and both the foundation for (Matt. 6:12,14; Mark 11:25; Luke 6:37) and response to the forgiveness of God (Eph. 4:32). Jesus urges us not only to forgive others but to make every effort to find forgiveness where another holds something against us (see Matt. 5:23–26).

There is no doubt that the ability to forgive and accept forgiveness is one of the hallmarks of maturity and it is a fundamental goal in counselling. So many who seek counsel, because of chronic anxiety, strained relationships or a tendency to depression, harbour a dilemma about forgiveness. They may find it virtually impossible to forgive or be forgiven.

Jane was someone locked into an inner prison which seemed to have no doors marked 'forgiveness'. Sexually abused at an early age, she could not bring herself to forgive her molesters. Until her anger and resentment towards men in general, as well as certain men in particular, could be listened to, understood and forgiven, she seemed imprisoned by her unforgiving spirit. Here was a desperate need to face the wounding past, to cry tears of anger and grief, to experience the forgiving and healing Lord at the centre of her being, and then to allow his forgiveness to spill over to those others who had offended. Jane could not – and indeed none of us could in similar circumstances – forgive such enormity without entering into the pain of recollection and its resulting hurt, sustained by the God who forgives and makes all things new. This path of repentance within the counselling process is never easy, but through it the forgiven and forgiving can come into a country where, once more, the life-giving balance between responsibility and freedom can hold sway. Lawrence Crabb writes:

> It is through deep repentance . . . that God is enjoyed and people are loved. Forgiveness of those who hurt and movement in whatever direction obedience requires are built on the foundation of repentance. The result is a deeper awareness of Christ's love for us and the value we have in His plan for touching others.[4]

The Greek word *aphiemi*, to forgive, used in the Bible, is made up from *apo*, 'from', and *hiemi*, 'to send'. This idea of 'to send from' or 'to let go' is intrinsic to the concept of forgiveness. We see this in the Jubilee year, 'the Lord's time for cancelling debts' (Deut. 15:2), when God's people were required to 'let go' of any debts owed to them. This same principle is written into the very notion of forgiveness, as Jesus made abundantly clear in his model prayer to the Father: 'Forgive us our debts, as we also have forgiven our debtors' (Matt. 6:12). We can say that to forgive others is to release them from what they owe us and, thereby, to free them from our control.

So many who come for counselling struggle with the weight of what others owe them and, like Jane, they find it next to impossible to free others from their indebtedness. For Sally the sticking point was the possessiveness of her mother, for Neil it was the accidental death of his brother, for Ian it was the rejecting attitudes of his adoptive parents, and for Dora it was the many hard things her husband, Jack, had said over the long years of their marriage.

One of the greatest challenges in counselling is to listen patiently to the anguish felt by those who hold such deep-seated resentments. Often, they are telling their tale for the first time and the confession of anger and frustration can, in itself, begin to lessen the burden of guilt. There comes a point, however, when clients need to face the issue of forgiving others. Frequently, this also necessitates an awareness of the client's own need for forgiveness, for an unforgiving spirit is as culpable as the sins of the offending party. For Hilda, the negative attitudes she had held towards her authoritarian and dismissive father for years began to give way to greater understanding and warmer feelings following a time of shared praying with her counsellor. In such situations, progress may be slow since old wounds run deep. Sometimes, where the offender cannot be reached due to death or illness, the client is best helped by writing a letter which declares forgiveness; the letter is then destroyed and the matter laid to rest, with God's continuing help. At other times, and here the Lord's special grace will be needed, the client should be encouraged to take practical steps to demonstrate a change of heart. Through carefully chosen words, the carrying out of new loving actions and the avoidance of old, negative reactions, changed attitudes are shown and all parties are released from the baleful control of the past.

Friendship

A crucial aspect of the intermediate goal of reconciliation is friendship. It is my experience that in almost all counselling situations the person seen is one half of a significant relationship. This is, of course, at its most obvious in marital counselling and family therapy but, nonetheless, when seeing a client singly there is usually a spouse, a blood-relative, a lover, friend or colleague whose existence within the unfolding story is at times so powerful that the person seems to be present in the room. The 'empty chair' technique of Gestalt therapy, by allowing the client free rein to conduct a dialogue with the absent individual, is useful in helping a person face up to relational difficulties. From time to time, when counselling a husband or wife whose spouse refuses to attend, and where things are being said that seem harsh or dismissive, I have pointed to a neighbouring chair and said, 'Let's imagine your partner is sitting with us. Now continue to tell me about your relationship'. The acute awareness of the accused's imagined presence often does wonders for the tone and content of what is then said!

Where a couple can be seen together, as in marital counselling, the gradual taking up of fresh responsibility for their lives is likely to include the need to forgive each other and seek to re-establish their friendship. It is here that intermediate goals and programmes require clarification. The two individuals need to be encouraged, each in turn, to propose and discuss a realistic and achievable objective for the other partner to aim at during the coming week or two. Often, within marriage and other close relationships, the building blocks of reconciliation are quite modest. There is commonly less need for the grand gesture ('No, darling, a new car won't help – even if we could afford one!') than for a simple commitment to small practical details ('Yes, it would be good if you put up the shelf by Sunday', or 'Yes, I would like it if you looked at me more when we chatted'). There is also often less requirement for deeply significant conversation than for keeping in touch over thoughts, feelings, intentions and plans.

Many who seek direction and counsel, however, ache for friendships, even ones that have fallen apart and need repair. Some come for help due to inadequate social skills; others because low self-esteem and an insatiable desire to belong have pushed people away; yet others because their giftedness and competence is a threat which distances would-be friends.

It is not unusual for friendship to have an asymmetrical quality, its importance being greater for the one than the other. The friendship between J. R. R. Tolkien and C. S. Lewis had something of this element. Tolkien's marriage had major difficulties and, in 1929, he wrote in his diary, 'Friendship with Lewis compensates for much'. Lewis seemed less enamoured for, in 1931, in a letter to another acquaintance, he referred to Tolkien as 'one of my friends of the second class'![5]

Friendship is a neglected subject in many Christian circles, especially evangelical ones.[6] It is sad that an emphasis on marriage as the norm, and a suspicion of extended relationships amongst the single, has led, on the one hand, to a blinkered attitude over scriptural teaching on friendship and, on the other, to an ignorance (amongst the married!) of the realities of singleness. There is a profound need amongst Christians – not least in relation to trends towards later marriage – to re-establish the value of friendship, according to biblical principles.

The Book of Proverbs, for example, points out that friendship should be marked by loyalty ('there is a friend that sticks closer than a brother' [18:24]); by consistency ('A friend loves at all times' [17:17]); and by healthy exchange ('As iron sharpens iron, so one man sharpens another' [27:17]). There are a number of exemplary friendships within Scripture – between David and Jonathan, Ruth and Naomi, Paul and Timothy – but the most outstanding are seen in our Lord's relating to others. His circle of friends was wide and included many on the edge of society, for he was known as 'a friend of tax collectors and "sinners"' (Matt. 11:19). He also knew the importance of closer sets of friends of both sexes: as well as calling to himself the twelve – 'those he wanted . . . that they might be with him and that he might send them out' (Mark 3:13–14) – he also valued more intimate ties with Peter, James and John, with Mary Magdalene, and with the three from Bethany: Mary, Martha and Lazarus. He summed up the self-sacrifice and openness of all godly friendship in these words:

> My command is this: Love each other as I have loved you. Greater love has no-one than this, that he lay down his life for his friends. You are my friends if you do what I command. I no longer call you servants, because a servant does not know his master's business. Instead, I have called you friends, for everything that I learned from my Father I have made known to you. (John 15:12–15)

Jesus restored friendship to its rightful place as an expression of God-centred living. One of the main outcomes of pastoral care and counselling should be that such friendships, across the barriers of sex, class and race, are repaired, renewed or discovered for the first time.

There are many, though, for whom friendship remains elusive at certain stages of life – perhaps through bereavement, divorce, geographical distance or simply the parting of ways. At such times there is the need to journey from loneliness to solitude, from the heartache of isolation to the solace of being alone, and yet not alone. Jesus knew both loneliness and solitude. He experienced the desertion of friends but, in anticipating that loss, could also say, 'Yet I am not alone, for my Father is with me' (John 16:32). We know, too, that his sense of companionship with the Father was to be broken for three long hours when, engulfed by the darkness of humanity's sin, he cried out from the cross, 'My God, my God, why have you forsaken me?'

Here is the mystery and the wonder: Christ experienced the quintessence of loneliness so that we might never be alone. Henri Nouwen, reflecting on his seven-month stay in a Trappist monastery, points to companionship with Christ as the only valid resource for combating loneliness:

> In 1970 I felt so lonely that I could not give; now I feel so joyful that giving seems easy. I hope that the day will come when the memory of my present joy will give me the strength to keep giving even when loneliness gnaws at my heart. When Jesus was loneliest, he gave most. That realisation should help to deepen my commitment to service and let my desire to give become independent of my actual experience of joy. Only a deepening of my life in Christ will make that possible.[7]

There are, of course, many lonely people who seek counsel. They, like Nouwen, feel so lonely that they cannot give. The counsellor who will listen to their cry of loneliness, and, unlike many in their lives, will not step away, may become an important bridge towards future friendship. The counsellor cannot *supply* that friendship, because the consequent loss of objectivity will prevent the client from developing an understanding of the roots of his or her loneliness. As the counsellor stays the course and proves to be trustworthy, the client can take heart from this dependable relationship and begin to take risks in other social contexts. Where the client is also assured of the friendship of the Lord and his people, then the resources for a sense of belonging are limitless, however profound the former isolation.

And so, as we encourage one another to forgive and be forgiven, to befriend and receive friendship, and to journey from loneliness to solitude, let us ever be open to the God who delights to offer companionship on the way. As James Nelson has written:

> Surely, it is the friendship of God to which the Christian affirmation of grace points. If we say that God loves us, what

we are saying is that God confirms us, God confronts us, God celebrates us. And when we have experienced that kind of friendship, that kind of acceptance, even if momentarily, we know that everything is transformed and we can never be quite the same again.[8]

Freedom

Where responsibility ignores freedom it becomes hidebound and joyless: where freedom loses a sense of responsibility it becomes anarchic and selfish. The Bengali poet and philosopher, Rabindranath Tagore, paints a word-picture of a responsibility which is sensitive to the fulfilment of others, and finds its own freedom through letting go:

> The bow whispers to the arrow
> Ere it speeds forth:
> 'Thy freedom is my freedom'.[9]

Not only are responsibility and freedom intimately related, but the attainment of freedom can only be found through responsibility. One of the most powerful expressions of this view is found in these words of Jesus, spoken during an interchange with some Jews 'who had believed him':

If you hold to my teaching, you are really my disciples. Then you will know the truth, and the truth will set you free . . . I tell you the truth, everyone who sins is a slave to sin. Now a slave has no permanent place in the family, but a son belongs to it for ever. So if the Son sets you free, you will be free indeed. (John 8:31–36)

Here is the call to responsible living, to a life of obedience and discipline, a discipleship to Jesus which, in turn, liberates. A stark contrast is made between the state of being a 'slave to sin' – in which, at the extremes, the man or woman is bound to a loveless legalism or let loose into unbridled licence – and that of being a son or daughter, whose family likeness is shown in responsiveness to God and in a life marked by the freedom of the Son.

We have already seen how many who come for counselling are either bound by long-held resentment towards others or by profound feelings of isolation. In both cases, there is little sense of true freedom: the first is shackled by an unforgiving spirit, the second is hemmed in by loneliness. It is forgiveness and friendship which can begin to unlock the doors towards other people. In counselling, the need for a sense of freedom is rarely far below the surface: in the adolescent who yearns to break away from the control of repressive parents; in the depressed single mother who longs to escape from her demanding small children; in the middle-aged couple who, now their family has left home, are bored with each other and desire new partners. The challenge for the counsellor is to help people like these discover the way forward in terms of a freedom which is not impulsive and selfish, but is responsible towards God, others and the self.

We will consider the freedom that can result from counselling, and that is one of its goals, under two headings: *dependence on God* and *laughter*.

Dependence on God

That responsible living and true freedom are inextricably linked can be seen in the problems that arise in relation to human autonomy and dependence. In counselling, just as we find that an absent friend or partner commonly features in the client's story, we also discover that distortions in relationships with others are frequently present. Once more, we see the shadow of humanity's fall. Ever since the flight from Eden, men and women have gravitated towards either a controlling independence or a manipulative dependency in their relations with one another. According to genetic make-up and upbringing, to parental example and the influence of peer groups, many of us spend a great deal of time and energy either shaking off others, however politely, who come too near or drawing others closer, however subtly, to establish a network of support and reassurance. In both enterprises there is a bid for freedom: in the former, freedom from intrusion; in the latter, freedom from exclusion. In both instances, where the quest for autonomy or dependency is extreme, the pain of isolation or of rejection may cause the person to seek counselling.

Janine had difficulties in relating to those around her and became more and more excluded from the decisions and confidences of others. Bright and attractive, she had grown up as a single child heavily cosseted by her parents, who believed her giftedness would take the world by storm. It was a battle for her to leave the parental home for college and, eventually, for a responsible job in a distant city. She made her assertive mark wherever she went – in the office, at church, in the traffic, at her shared flat. Her desire to control everything and everyone around her, and, at the same time, to keep others at bay, never quite worked. Behind her tough and confident exterior, she longed for emotional closeness and a sense of belonging. Following a series of relationships that broke up before they had hardly begun, she sought counselling.

Nick had the opposite problem to Janine, though the outcome was similar. Although his mother had been caring and, perhaps, overprotective, his father, always a distant figure, had died when Nick was fifteen. Nick had a number of male friends during his teen years and early twenties, though he tended to be demanding of their attention and clinging if they seemed to lose interest in him. He was polite, eager to please and popular with older women. He became obsessed by a slightly older male colleague at the bank where they both worked and, finding he was shunned and even ridiculed for his advances, Nick became increasingly depressed. Feeling undervalued and fearing he was homosexual, he sought help from a counsellor.

The stories of Janine and Nick illustrate the basic human desire for separateness and connectedness. A great deal of counselling seeks to help people like them find this combined sense of individuality and connection with others in the solitude of God-dependence and the companionship of interdependence. Here, we are once more in the domain discussed in chapter two (see pp. 31–35), where we saw that the restoration of our image-bearing relates both to the centrality of God in our lives and to our 'one-anotherness'. Jesus, who declared, 'I do nothing on my own but speak just what the Father has taught me' (John. 8:28), and urged his followers to love one another, is our model.

Most, if not all, of us have difficulty over this call to Father-dependence and interdependence. Our human nature rebels against the notion that obedience to God and a caring involvement in the lives of others is the route to freedom. We find it hard to believe the paradox that whoever loses his or her life for Christ's sake will find it, and that laying up treasure in heaven is such a good idea when all kinds of earthly treasures beckon. We seem to prefer a semblance of freedom, which is really slavery, to a service that is perfect freedom. Lawrence Crabb is realistic about this dilemma when he writes:

> Image-bearers can handle their longings in only one of two ways: Either we can turn to God and cling with stubborn intensity to Him when life threatens to rip out our very souls, or we can deny the depth and meaning of our pain and keep on working to feel better without sacrificing our independence. None of us perfectly elects the first choice and most don't even consider it.[10]

One of the most crucial goals within the counselling process, therefore, is to encourage a deeper dependence on God and a profounder commitment to others. For Janine, counselling helped her to see that her bid to control those around her tended to distance her from the warmth of human relating. She needed both to be more vulnerable with others, admitting her fallibility where appropriate, and to listen more carefully to God's direction for her life. In fact, as she developed a regular time of quiet reflection and prayer at the beginning of each day, trusting God more fully with the day's decisions and relationships, she found she was less inclined to manipulate the lives of those around her and began to taste the delights of one or two closer friendships.

For Nick, a more protracted stretch of counselling proved necessary in order to help him on the road to a right sense of separateness and connectedness. His homosexual leanings were deepseated and found to be linked with a lack of a strong and admired father-figure in his childhood. In fact, he found it hard to give any real impression of what sort of man his father had been. His tendency to form highly dependent relationships with male friends arose out of a childhood impoverished of male closeness. Gradually, through experiencing a relationship of trust and non-possessive warmth (see pp. 98–102) with his male counsellor, he became less clinging and demanding in his same-sex friendships. At least one relationship with a man was proving safe and worthwhile and so, wondered Nick, perhaps others could be too. At the same time, his growing appreciation of a loving God, whose compassion far exceeded that of any earthly father or mother, helped to give him a sense of stability beyond himself and his everyday relationships.

I like the story of Francis of Assisi, the 'tumbler for God', who, when tempted to pride, would stand on his head in order to gain a right perspective. The word 'dependent' means 'hanging' and he would thus view his beloved city as if it were suspended from above, its very existence reliant on divine mercy. As G. K. Chesterton put it: 'Instead of being merely proud of his strong city . . . he would be thankful to God Almighty that it had not been dropped'![11] Both Janine and Nick, with their opposite dilemmas of proud autonomy and a childish dependency, found a new taste of freedom in a deeper reliance on God. There is no need to suggest to clients that, with Francis of Assisi, they worship God upside-down, but our prayer should be that we would all see life in a new way, aware of our dependence on a God who cares and is merciful. Therein lies our freedom:

It is for freedom that Christ has set us free. Stand firm, then, and do not let yourselves be burdened again by a yoke of slavery. (Gal. 5:1)

Laughter

It may seem strange to declare that laughter, as an expression of freedom, is an intermediate goal in counselling. And yet, where, within the counselling process, someone formerly gloomy, defeated and joyless breaks into a laughter that is not cynical or bitter, then I am encouraged to believe that some freeing of the spirit may be taking place. This is the sort of laughter that Turgenev spoke of when he said, 'When you laugh you forgive and are ready to love'.[12] Such laughter is not cruel or vindictive, amused by another's misfortune, but arises out of relief that a particular crisis is past or some new insight has been gained or, perhaps best of all, where the client is able to laugh at himself or herself.

The Bible says little about such laughter directly, but it is hard to believe that all it contains about rejoicing, praise and being blessed does not include the wondrous sound of the saints laughing. Mingle with any group of Christians where the Holy Spirit is clearly at work, breaking down barriers and releasing people from guilt and tension, and laughter will soon be heard. When God brings freedom, laughter is never far away:

When the Lord brought back the captives to Zion, we were like men who dreamed. Our mouths were filled with laughter, our tongues with songs of joy. Then it was said among the nations, 'The Lord has done great things for them'. The Lord has done great things for us, and we are filled with joy. (Ps. 126:1–3)

Something of this holy mirth is recorded by Harry Williams in an address for Lent he preached in 1980 at St James's, Piccadilly. Speaking on the value of humour, he recalled a story about two of the Knox brothers on a visit to see the third brother,

Wilfred, who was dying in Addenbrooke's hospital, Cambridge. Hearing a roar of laughter from the two visitors, the ward sister remonstrated with them, saying, 'You shouldn't laugh, that man is dying'. One of the brothers replied, 'But he is going to God'. However, the ward sister did not seem to equate God with merriment and said firmly, 'There is no need to bring in blasphemy as well'![13]

Stephen Pattison has pointed out the link between failure and laughter: an awareness of personal sin and weakness can lead, as relief from guilt is experienced, to a laughter that heals. One couple, setting up home around small children, found themselves bickering over practical priorities. He felt strongly that external structural matters had to be dealt with first; she longed for the completion of a long-promised set of kitchen cupboards. It was their ability to laugh during a counselling session – she at her persistence and he at his own ruses to avoid DIY indoors – that indicated their ability to admit faults and make amends. Pattison rightly sees that pastoral care has the common touch where there are tears and laughter:

> Failure and laughter go to the root of what it is to be human. They also lie close to some of the most important insights of theology. Failure is a place where people are most aware of the senselessness of sin and evil. It is a condition from which they most want to be saved. Laughter as its counterpart provides an experience of grace, hope and creative possibility as well as profound human solidarity . . . Laughter and tears lie at the heart of pastoral encounters and relationships. They must find a much more prominent place in fundamental thinking and writing about the nature of pastoral care as well.[14]

In counselling, where laughter and tears are indicators of new insights into the human condition, we can sense that people are on the road towards a greater responsibility and a fuller appreciation of freedom. As the imprisoning elements in their lives – age-old resentments, wilful independence and clinging dependencies – are listened to, challenged, repented of and forgiven, the fresh, liberating air of God's love and strength can enter, open the prison doors and bring release. It is not surprising that such times of refreshment and liberation are accompanied by the tears of penitence and the laughter of a new awakening.

The intermediate goals of pastoral care and counselling – a greater sense of responsibility in daily living, deeper reconciliation in all human relating and a fuller freedom in trusting and serving God – can be seen within the orbit of the great mission of Christ, summed up in the messianic declaration:

> The Spirit of the Sovereign Lord is on me, because the Lord has anointed me to preach good news to the poor. He has sent me to bind up the broken-hearted, to proclaim freedom for the captives and release from darkness for the prisoners, to proclaim the year of the Lord's favour . . . to comfort all who mourn . . . to bestow on them a crown of beauty instead of ashes, the oil of gladness instead of mourning, and a garment of praise instead of a spirit of despair. They will be called oaks of righteousness, a planting of the Lord for the display of his splendour. (Isa. 61:1–3)

Questions for Discussion

1. Pool ideas on what you see as the ultimate aims in counselling. (You might refer here to your discussions at the end of the previous chapter). Discuss interim goals that might be sought with these overall aims in mind.
2. Here is a case-study you might like to look at in order to focus on the setting of goals, and programmes for achieving them.

Roland and Rowena

Roland (thirty-five) and Rowena (thirty-two) have been married six years and have two children: Tamsyn (four) and Timothy (two). All four grandparents are alive, though Rowena's parents were divorced when she was fifteen and both remarried; she has hardly seen her father since his second marriage soon after her eighteenth birthday. Roland's parents live nearby and he has a particularly close relationship with his mother. He works as an accountant in a small firm of partners in a nearby town. Rowena trained as a nurse and would like to return to this work as soon as possible. Both are members of a local church and it has become obvious to many there that the marriage is under considerable strain. A recent episode between them at a church meeting, when Rowena stormed out, caused quite a stir. The couple have come to you for counsel.

Over two or three sessions at weekly intervals you discover that Rowena is frustrated by the demands of the children and feels that Roland takes next to no part in the practicalities of their upbringing. She longs to have some space for herself and for developing outside friendships and interests. She has looked for a father-figure in marrying Roland and has been disappointed. Roland is angry at Rowena's demands and feels he does his bit by occasionally taking the children out on Saturday mornings. His involvement with the local church is considerable and he feels that is a right priority. He sees a lot of his mother and resents Rowena's dismissal of her as an 'interfering old busybody'; he cannot see why Rowena will not take up his mother's offer to have the children for an occasional weekend.

Discuss possible goals, and programmes for achieving those goals, for Rowena and Roland. In reality, agreed goals and programmes would be arrived at as a three-cornered discussion involving clients and counsellor. Keep in mind the following:

a. Think of all the possible aspects of their situation, including: people, places, organisations, influences, attitudes, interests, priorities, employment, use of time.

b. Generate as many ideas as you can – even wild ones!

c. Try to be specific and practical in your suggestions.

d. Try to keep to what is achievable over (i) one month; (ii) six months.

3. Discuss the feelings that the story of Roland and Rowena generated in you and try to understand why you reacted as you did.

Personal Reflection

Spend some time in prayer and silent reflection on the next six months of your life. Whatever your situation now, try to see how it will be for you then.

Turn a piece of paper (preferably A4) sideways so that the greater length is horizontal. Divide the surface into three vertical columns titled, from left to right, 'area of life', 'goals' and 'programmes'. Subdivide the 'area of life' column horizontally into 'relating to others', 'work and creativity' and 'personal growth'.

Take some time to write out specific goals you would like to see achieved in your life by the end of six months in each of these areas. (Even if you do not have paid employment, still tackle the section on 'work and creativity'.) Do not be too ambitious – it is best if the goals are actually achievable!

Then consider the programmes for achieving your intended goals and write those down too, e.g. if your goal under 'relating to others' is to 'forgive my friend for letting me down', then you need to think of practicalities, like (a) 'phone her when she comes back from holiday and arrange for her to come round for coffee'; (b) 'pray like mad about the meeting'; and (c) 'take the plunge'.

Having completed the form, commit your resolves to God and seek to implement them during the coming weeks and months. Keep the list and refer back to it from time to time.

9

The Bible and Counselling Today

My soul is weary with sorrow; strengthen me according to your word.

Psalm 119:28

One of the exercises I use in training counsellors is to hold up a house brick and ask, 'How many uses can you think of for this brick?' I have asked this question many times now and am still discovering new ideas! A similar question about the Bible might, depending on the gathering, meet with a similar variety: door-stop, stepping stone, book-end, paper-weight, draught-excluder, support for a chair, table or bed where one leg is too short, an ornament, a seat . . .

There is, of course, more to it than that and the Bible can be an invaluable tool in counselling. Nonetheless the stories of many lives abound with instances where the Scriptures have been misused or even abused. One of the tragedies within the rise of the secular psychologies has been the way the inadequate use and understanding of the Bible has contributed to the agnostic and atheistic beliefs of many influential therapists and counsellors. Carl Rogers, for example, grew up in a family with fundamentalist Christian views, where the Protestant work ethic was rated highly and neighbours were shunned because of their dubious morals and ways of living. It is interesting to reflect on the probable link between his mother's two favourite biblical maxims ('Come out from among them and be ye separate', 'All our righteousness is as filthy rags in thy sight, O Lord') and Rogers' later emphases on open communication with everyone and the notion that within each person are all the resources needed for growth and change.[1]

Whereas Carl Rogers' experience was of a background that overemphasised certain scriptural texts to the neglect of other perspectives, such as the compassion and mercy of God, Karen Horney, the psychoanalyst, grew up in the equally negative atmosphere of inconsistency between belief and practice. Although teaching the family the Christian faith, her parents had a stormy marriage and her father, a Danish sea captain, earned the nickname 'Bible-thrower' due to his violent misuse of the Scriptures!

How, then, are we to use the Bible in our caring and counselling? Is it right to quote texts to people in need? Should we always have an open Bible at hand? If we are to share the Scriptures, which parts are most suitable in a counselling relationship? What are the links between the Bible and prayer, listening, silence, the imagination, and the work of the Holy Spirit? Or is the open use of the Bible so controversial or potentially harmful that it is best kept out of sight, if not out of mind? It will help to take a quick look at the range of emphases and styles in using the Scriptures found in the various sectors of pastoral care and counselling. Since there are limited ways of approaching people in need, it should not be a surprise that the four psychological systems of behaviourism, psychoanalysis, personalism and transpersonalism are reflected in the four main strands of Christian caring and counselling. We can describe these approaches as *cognitive-behavioural; analytic; Christian personalist* and *Christian transpersonalist* – each tending towards its own distinctive way of handling the Bible.

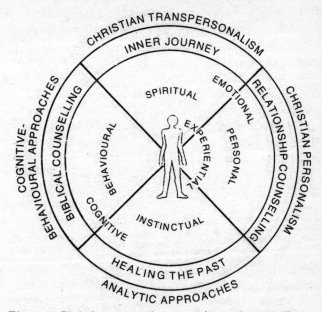

Figure 3. Christian approaches to caring and counselling.

As we consider each of these in turn, we will find that cognitive-behavioural approaches (often termed 'biblical' counselling) are primarily prophetic in emphasis and prescriptive in their use of the Bible (I will argue below that they would be better called 'prophetic' counselling); analytic approaches look to the healer and the 'wise', tending to be reflective and 'visionary'; Christian personalist methods are pastoral and formative; and Christian transpersonalist approaches are priestly and imaginative (see figure 4). It is not, however, as simple as that, and the diagrams can only be approximations of how things are: reality is always more complex and less predictable! Just to take one example, Christian personalists, who stress the importance of the counselling relationship, may well, from time to time, use the Bible prescriptively, reflectively or imaginatively.

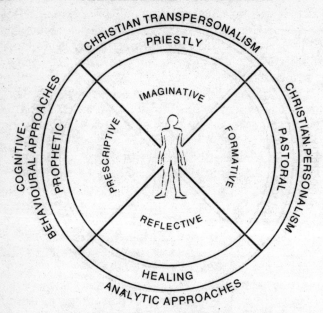

Figure 4. The use of the Bible in counselling.

Cognitive-Behavioural Approaches

Lionel, a single man in his mid-thirties, had been a Christian for many years when he first sought counselling. He was clearly diffident about why he had come but, in time, admitted that he was virtually obsessed by his habit of frequent masturbation. He had quite recently taken to buying magazines of soft pornography and was full of guilty feelings about his sexual fantasies. Although he had been lonely in the past, he now had a caring relationship with a young woman from the church he attended and, within this friendship, felt even more ashamed of his secretive habits. There is no doubt that he was greatly helped by simply sharing his anxieties but, from an early stage in counselling, he clearly needed strategies to help him regain his self-respect. It was through reflecting on biblical passages that teach clearly that God calls us to give every aspect of our lives, including our sexuality, to him, that Lionel began to gain victory. In learning such texts as, 'Do you not know that your body is a temple of the Holy Spirit?' (1 Cor. 6:19) and, '. . . if anything is excellent or praiseworthy – think about such things' (Phil. 4:8), and recalling them at times of temptation, he found not only substantial improvement in his thought-world and actions but also in his attitudes and relationships.

Amongst evangelical Christians there are a number of approaches to counselling which, as in Lionel's story, stress the importance of right thinking and right behaviour. Such methodologies find good scriptural precedent for their emphasis, for example: 'I have hidden your word in my heart that I might not sin against you' (Ps. 119:11) and 'Be transformed by the renewing of your mind' (Rom. 12:2). Approaches which incorporate these and similar perspectives (without necessarily excluding other dimensions of a person's life, such as the emotions) include Larry Crabb's biblical counselling, Jay Adams' nouthetic counselling, Martin and Deirdre Bobgans' spiritual counselling, Selwyn Hughes' Christian counselling and Gary Collins' discipleship counselling.

Within such methodologies, the prophetic element often predominates in that exhortation, admonition, confrontation and the call to repentance are frequently present. As we saw in chapter five (see pp. 79–81), the call of the prophet was typically to the people of God, and Christian cognitive-behavioural approaches function primarily within pastoral settings. It is in this sector that the term 'biblical' counselling is frequently used and, as I mentioned earlier, the phrase 'prophetic' counselling seems to me to be more appropriate. The adjective 'biblical' suggests that only this counselling method is true to biblical revelation. There are a number of strands within pastoral care and counselling, representing different aspects of the ways in which people can find Christ-centred help. No one sector can claim the prerogative over the Bible and its use. While the cognitive-behavioural sector does stress the use of Scripture most strongly, the essence of this sector consists in the prophetic element in helping others.

Jay Adams' nouthetic counselling is a prime example of this focus: it concentrates on the concepts expressed by the verb *noutheteo* (to warn, admonish, advise), and the equivalent noun, *nouthesia* – New Testament words which are always used within the context of Christian fellowship. It is here that we are reminded of the call of instruct one another (Rom. 15:14), the need to learn from the sins of the past (1 Cor. 10:11) and to submit to the authority of Church leaders (Rom. 15:14; 1 Cor. 4:14; 1 Thes. 5:12; 2 Thes. 3:15), and the links between warning and teaching in the growth towards Christian maturity (Col. 1:28; 3:16).

There is, of course, a wider brief to the prophetic element in counselling than brotherly and sisterly admonition. The prophet is one who is led and inspired by the Holy Spirit, who proclaims restoration and liberation, as well as judgment and captivity. Cognitive-behavioural approaches that are true to the Bible should, therefore, be open to the Holy Spirit's promptings and the hopefulness of God's compassionate dealings. This will involve the counsellor being God-directed, as well as directing others; submitting to the Lord's authority, as well as exercising an authoritative style; and being someone who brings hope, as well as challenge and confrontation. Stephen Pattison is rightly critical of a truncated Pauline theology where the importance of the 'mind' (*nous*) is over-stressed. He writes:

> What is called for is a transformation of a person's whole being and behaviour in obedience to the presence of the reality of God. For Paul himself the *nous* element of a person needs to be subordinated to the Spirit, *pneuma*. Counselling which claims to be based on Paul's theology would be better entitled 'pneumatic counselling'![2]

Where cognitive-behavioural approaches amongst Christians tend to be prophetic in style, they are also inclined to use the Scriptures prescriptively. An analogy could be made here to a doctor's prescribing habits, in that a diagnosis is made ('This client is clearly suffering from laziness.') and treatment is prescribed ('Mend your ways, learn Hebrews 6:12: "We do not want you to become lazy, but to imitate those who through faith and patience inherit what has been promised." See me again in a week's time.'). Although it is easy to parody this method, we do find some parallels within the Scriptures. Psalm 119, for instance, is an extended celebration of the wonder and prescriptive power of what God says and commands:

How can a young man keep his way pure?
By living according to your word.
I seek you with all my heart;
do not let me stray from your commands.
I have hidden your word in my heart
that I might not sin against you. (Ps. 119:9–11)

We have, too, the example of Jesus, who was clearly deeply versed in the Old Testament and quoted from its pages on many occasions. During the temptations in the wilderness, in the extremis of his hunger and physical weakness, he counters the Enemy's attack with biblical statements culled from his meditations on the Book of Deuteronomy.[3]

The learning, remembering and application of relevant biblical verses is an important technique in counselling that parallels the 'changing the tapes' concept of cognitive-behavioural therapy. In this context, Epictetus, the Stoic philosopher, is readily quoted. He wrote: 'Men are disturbed not by things, but by the views which they take of them'. Cognitive approaches to counselling argue that irrational beliefs need to be recognised and countered by more realistic assessments, so that negative behaviour gives way to more socially acceptable responses.[4]

Albert Ellis has put forward his ABC model as a way of outlining the counterproductive cycle of negative thinking.[5] In this cycle, an Activating event (A) is misinterpreted by mistaken

Beliefs (B), thus producing negative emotional and behavioural Consequences (C). We might take the example of a young man who, one day, is ignored by a colleague when they pass in the corridor at their workplace. This is the Activating event and, because the young man has the Belief that all his closer contacts eventually give up on him, the Consequences for him are emotional dejection and avoidance of the colleague, for fear of further snubbing. Even though the reality might have been that the colleague was simply preoccupied by his thoughts on the day in question, or feeling anti-social due to chronic indigestion, the young man pursues his inner statement ('I am hopeless and not worth knowing') and outer behaviour ('Because contact is painful, I'll avoid others in future').

Cognitive-behavioural counselling seeks to help such a client to weigh up his maladaptive ways and so discover and substitute more realistic thinking about everyday events. Within a Christian context, the young man might be shown from the Scriptures that he is valued by God, that his sins can be forgiven and that he is to love others, including his colleague. Discussion of such biblical insights might lead, in turn, to the giving of an assignment, or 'homework', in which the client learns and writes out on a card the text: 'I can do everything through him [the Lord] who gives me strength' (Phil. 4:13). During the week or so between counselling sessions, whenever the young man finds he is about to say to himself, 'I am worthless', he is to 'change the tape' by referring to the statement from Philippians. It is argued that such an inner declaration will lead to different feelings and actions towards others. He might, for example, find himself saying to his colleague, 'I noticed you looked quite preoccupied yesterday. Is everything OK for you?' Such an enquiry, where genuine, could prove a valuable building block in a more realistic and caring relationship.

Hebrews 4:12 declares that the word of God is 'living and active', and 'sharper than any double-edged sword', and it is salutary to remember that the Bible is likened to a potentially lethal weapon! There is a danger in cognitive-behavioural approaches, with their prophetic stance and prescriptive use of Scripture, that people in need can be badly damaged by insensitive or overzealous handling of the word of God. I sometimes wonder whether Christians who counsel should put a large notice on the cover of their Bible: THIS BOOK IS DANGEROUS. HANDLE WITH CARE! As Gary Sweeten has put it, the Bible may be the 'sword of the Spirit', but we are not to wield it to 'perform open heart surgery' at every turn – a heavy-handed approach to people that 'exudes death'.[6]

However, it is far from inevitable that prophetic counselling needs to bludgeon needy people with the word of God. Within this sector, exhortation, advice giving and appropriate confrontation, as we saw with Lionel's story, can all play their constructive part where the Scriptures are handled with discernment. When prophetic counsellors, emphasising the need to change patterns of thinking and behaviour according to biblical guidelines, do so with compassion and sensitivity, guided and empowered by the Holy Spirit, then God's word can most readily exercise its challenging and restorative work.

Analytic Approaches

The 'archaeological dig' of psychoanalytic therapy, with its painstaking unveiling of layer after layer of the human psyche, is paralleled in much Christian counselling by the notion of the 'journey back'. Methods such as prayer counselling, healing of the memories, faith imagination, primal integration, with its focus on reliving intra-uterine and perinatal experiences, and the healing of the family tree, seek to track down and bring peace to the traumas of earlier existence.[7] Whereas cognitive-behavioural approaches focus on the conscious realm of thinking and action, this analytic section of 'inner healing' concentrates on those experiences and memories that have been locked away in the unconscious.[8] It is interesting to note that a significant number of 'journey-back' methodologies, in contrast to those in the other three sectors, have been pioneered by women. Just as names such as Anna Freud, Melanie Klein and Karen Horney figure prominently in the story of psychoanalytic thought and practice, so, in the Christian world of inner healing, outstanding names include Agnes Sanford, Anne White, Catherine Marshall, Ruth Carter Stapleton and Flora Slosson Wuellner. The reasons for this are, I suspect, many. Negatively, they may include a reflection, historically, of male bias and dominance within the essentially cerebral activity of systematising methodologies. More positively, it seems that the 'feminine' attributes of sensitivity, perceptiveness, intuition and genuine feeling (all neglected by the stereotypical male of Western society) are especially needed in bringing healing to the wounded and release to the bound. It is women, in particular, (and certain men who are in touch with the 'feminine' within) who have been in the forefront of the 'journey back' concept, exploring what is hidden, forgotten and repressed.

Where the exhortatory and admonishing style of Christian cognitive-behavioural approaches looks primarily to the role of the prophet, the quest for 'inner healing' particularly draws on the gifts and qualities of the healer and the 'wise one' (see pp. 83–86). Godly wisdom has a wide range of application within caring and counselling and the Bible stresses both its origin 'from above' and its effects, through proverbial insight, in everyday situations. It is the former of these aspects, with its emphasis on the Holy Spirit's intervention, that is the mainspring of this sector's stress on healing and integration.

It is more difficult to be precise about the use of the Scriptures in this analytic approach. Whereas the prophetic style tends to be proclamatory and prescriptive in its handling of biblical texts, the healer's prime concern is to hear and respond to the Spirit's promptings in and through the written word. We might call this use of Scripture 'visionary', since its focus is on discernment, insight and seeing. Moreover, where cognitive-behavioural approaches tend to use the Bible deductively (reasoning from general scriptural statements and applying them in specific situations), methodologies seeking inner healing are inclined to handle Scripture inductively (seeing its value in certain instances and thus drawing general conclusions).[9]

Supposing a married woman comes for counselling and it is established that she has low self-esteem and feels so unloved by her husband that she is tempted to have an affair. A deductive and prescriptive approach is likely, sooner or later, to challenge her with a clear biblical statement – perhaps, quite simply, 'You shall not commit adultery' (Exod. 20:14). The reasoning, in effect, is: 'The Bible has made clear the general principle that adultery is always wrong. This woman is tempted to be unfaithful to her husband and so is in danger of breaking God's commandment. I must urge her, through an appropriate text, to refrain from sin.' Here the focus is to replace wrong thinking and behaviour with right thinking and behaviour.

Although a biblically based approach to inner healing will have a similar concern to prevent the folly of an adulterous relationship, it is likely that the use of the Bible will be different. Since attention will be given to the hidden past as well as the known present, there will be a concern to open up the woman's poor self-image to the Spirit's forgiving, accepting and healing action. The counsellor might recall, for example, that on a number of occasions Psalm 139 has proved especially helpful to those battling with poor self-esteem. It might be suggested to the woman that she reflect on verses fourteen to sixteen, seeking the Holy Spirit's insight:

> I praise you because I am fearfully and wonderfully made;
> your works are wonderful, I know that full well.
> My frame was not hidden from you
> when I was made in the secret place.
> When I was woven together in the depths of the earth,
> your eyes saw my unformed body.
> All the days ordained for me were written in your book
> before one of them came to be.

Out of this inductive and reflective approach God may speak very powerfully to the client of his love for her, at a level that touches the very roots of her existence within the womb and in early childhood. One young woman I sought to help in this way had a deep experience of the Father's tender acceptance of her through these verses, although she could not, at that point, see that 'all the days ordained' for her 'were written in [God's] book' (v. 16). The idea that God's loving hand had been part of the shaping of her story proved more elusive than the arresting awareness of his affirmation of her as a person he had made. The counsellor intent on inner healing must be prepared to be patient and trust God's timing, as he unfolds his work of integration stage by stage.

Just as a prescriptive method of handling Scripture can be in danger of heavy-handedness, so this more visionary and reflective style can, at times, sit too loose to the context and content of a passage. Some proponents of inner healing tend to view the Bible as a medium through which the Spirit may or may not speak, rather than as the word of God with its own intrinsic value and validity. Here we are back to the debate on how we should understand the inspiration of the Scriptures (see pp. 7–10) or, rather, how we are to comprehend the interplay between Spirit and word.

This is not a discussion that is easy to resolve but there is little doubt that much counselling is blighted, on the one hand, by a hard-edged emphasis on the written word that tends towards aridity and judgmentalism and, on the other hand, by a type of experience-centred stress on the Holy Spirit that leads to emotional instability and doctrinal looseness. As a counter to these poles of biblicism and subjectivism, Richard Lovelace has written:

The written Word and its doctrinal derivatives are not the sword of the Spirit unless his hand is upon them, and they are being wielded at his direction . . . The general precondition of live orthodoxy is the presence of the Holy Spirit, endorsing and applying sound doctrine, using at least minimal relevant quanta of biblical truth to realise the life of Christ in believers.[10]

It is a realisation of this 'life of Christ in believers', through the work of the Holy Spirit illuminating God's revealed truth, that is the aim of all Christian approaches to caring and counselling which seek to be Bible-based. Where the 'journey back' is pursued prayerfully, with due attention to biblical perspectives and the leading of the Spirit, then the healing hand of Christ can be brought to the dark and hidden places.

Christian Personalism

Given the Bible's teaching on the God who is three persons in one, the creation of humankind for relationship and the value of both individual and community, it comes as no surprise to find that personalism is an important sector in Christian counselling. Here, albeit with profound differences in their world-views, there are certain parallels with the humanistic and existential psychologies (see p. 50), in that the focus is on relationship. Within Christian personalism, counselling not only respects the uniqueness of the person being helped but also observes and utilises the relationship between client and counsellor, in order to overcome blocks to growth and maturity. Paul Tournier's 'dialogue' counselling and Howard Clinebell's 'growth' counselling are prime examples of this emphasis.[11]

So far, we have seen the focus on prophet and healer in Christian counselling, bringing change in thinking and behaviour, and inner healing respectively. Now, in Christian personalism, the stress is more on the shepherd – or, more fully, on the pastoral and paracletic – and the direction is essentially towards the achievement of maturity.

We saw in chapter five (pp. 87–88) something of the nurturing, protective, leading and courageous qualities of Jesus the Good

Shepherd – qualities which engender trust and an appropriate sense of security and significance. These pastoral elements should be the hallmark of the Christian 'relationship' counsellor. It is in this sector, in contrast to the 'prophetic' counselling of the cognitive-behavioural approaches, that we can use the term 'pastoral counselling.'[12]

There is, however, an extension of these pastoral characteristics in another biblical picture – that of the Paraclete, a term used of both Jesus and the Holy Spirit. The Paraclete is the one called, or sent, alongside the needy, the one who provides active help, who pleads the cause of, and intercedes for, those in desperate straits. And, in the discourse with his followers in the upper room,[13] Jesus talks of going away so that the Father might send the Holy Spirit, the second Paraclete, who will be available to all God's people in life's ups and downs:

And I will ask the Father, and he will give you another Counsellor (*parakletos*) to be with you for ever – the Spirit of truth. The world cannot accept him, because it neither sees him nor knows him. But you know him, for he lives with you and will be in you. I will not leave you as orphans; I will come to you. (John 14:16–18)

Although we have followed Firet in seeing the whole of the Church's work of pastoral care as a paracletic ministry (see pp. 43–44), it is in 'relationship' counselling that the various meanings of *parakaleo* come into their own. This Greek verb, which is frequently used in the New Testament (together with the noun *paraklesis*), is closely linked with the idea of the Paraclete, and has a range of meanings associated with caring for others. In the synoptic Gospels and the Book of Acts it often has the sense of asking, imploring or requesting in order to meet a human need, as when the Jewish leaders 'pleaded earnestly' with Jesus to come and heal the centurion's servant (Luke 7:4). A second meaning, 'to exhort', has some overlap with the challenging tone of *noutheteo* where 'exhortation' is understood as a call to fellow-believers to respond obediently to God's directives. Colin Brown puts it this way:

> . . . to exhort means to exert influence upon the will and decisions of another with the object of guiding him into a generally accepted code of behaviour or of encouraging him to observe certain instructions. Exhortation always presupposes some previous knowledge. It consists of reminding a person of this with the intention that he should carry it out. To exhort is to address the whole man.[14]

The third cluster of meanings of *parakaleo* includes 'to comfort', 'console' and 'encourage'. Here, the distressed, the afflicted, and the bereaved, are to receive strength, consolation and encouragement. Jesus declares such strengthening for those who grieve: 'Blessed are those who mourn, for they will be comforted' (Matt. 5:4), and Paul writes that his 'joy was greater than ever' (2 Cor. 7:7) because of the encouragement and comfort received from Titus and his news of the Christians in Corinth. Perhaps the clearest declaration, though, of *parakaleo*, and its relevance for Christian caring, is seen in 2 Corinthians 1:3–5:

> Praise be to the God and Father of our Lord Jesus Christ, the Father of compassion and the God of all comfort, who comforts us in all our troubles, so that we can comfort those in any trouble with the comfort we ourselves have received from God. For just as the sufferings of Christ flow over into our lives, so also through Christ our comfort overflows.

Here is the paracletic God who consoles and strengthens his troubled people, so that they, in turn, might bring solace to others. The channel of suffering and comfort runs from Christ to his followers and so to other needy people. Christ, the 'Wounded Healer',[15] the Suffering Servant, the one who knows the depths of affliction first-hand, comes alongside the sufferer to encourage and cheer.[16] He or she, through friendship or in the context of caring and counselling, thus becomes a 'missionary of comfort'.

The links between this sector of counselling and the Bible have been seen in the way the Scriptures undergird the notion of paracletic caring. Although the Christian personalist is open to using God's word prescriptively, as in cognitive-behavioural approaches, or reflectively, as in the 'journey back', the finely balanced nature of 'relationship' counselling may, for much of the time, preclude the open use of biblical texts. The focus is on the person in need and, though it is likely that specific matters of faith and commitment will be considered at some stage or other, the 'relationship' counsellor will be especially aware of the potentially distancing effect of the open Bible.

For some people, the idea of a method of Christian counselling in which the Bible may or may not figure directly is extremely suspect. However, it is important to see that such an approach, with its sensitivity to the fragility of human relating, that between counsellor and client included, can be truly biblical. Here we have the 'formative' use of Scripture,[17] in which the Bible itself forms, or shapes, every aspect of the counselling encounter – its presuppositions, aims, methods, process and relationship. Just as Jesus did not quote the Old Testament in each and every dialogue with others and yet always related to others according to the Father's will, so we need a similar discernment and power of discrimination.

Many Christians, of course, exercise their counselling skills within the community rather than in the pastoral settings of the local church or a Christian counselling organisation. Whether the context is one of the caring professions – such as social worker, nurse, teacher, clinical psychologist, probation officer, psychiatrist, general practitioner or practice counsellor – or within a business, voluntary agency or secular counselling organisation, it is entirely appropriate, I would argue, for the Christian to be true to the biblical revelation within a 'formative' style of counselling. Unlike the prescriptive and visionary use of the

Scriptures, which is explicit, the formative approach is *implicit*, allowing the Bible to work, yeast-like, within the dough of the counselling relationship.

There is, of course, the danger of imbalance in each of these sectors. We have seen how a heavy-handed use of Scripture or an approach that sits loose to the biblical text can spoil the legitimate emphases of prophetic counselling and inner healing respectively. In Christian personalism the temptation is to allow the implicit use of the Bible to slip into a loss of the biblical perspective, where, for example, the counsellor becomes weak on the seriousness of sin and falls into a 'universalism' that believes that everyone will, somehow or other, be part of the Kingdom. However, these errors are by no means inevitable.

Let me illustrate these points from my own experience of working in both pastoral and communal settings. As a Church leader with known pastoral gifts, in a large, suburban church, I am frequently asked to counsel fellow-Christians. Here the context is the fellowship of the people of God and both the client and I have that understanding. Within this framework, having listened carefully to the client to gauge his or her story, priorities and beliefs, it is often entirely appropriate for us to refer to a Bible passage. In doing this, my approach may be prescriptive, where the client needs challenge or encouragement in terms of thinking or behaviour, or reflective, where, prayerfully, we are seeking to listen to God for greater wisdom and to experience his healing power.

In contrast, although I am arguing that the approach is equally true to the Bible, when I work in communal settings in general practice, student health or psychiatry, my use of the Scriptures is implicit and formative. Here, I seek to relate to the patient as a fellow human being who, like me, has been created in God's image, is fallen and is redeemable in Christ. Further, I see the counselling or psychotherapy I offer in terms of Christ's call to love my neighbour as myself. These aspects of my biblical world-view help to shape my attitudes, manner and style of relating. However, where, in a communal setting, I refuse to take advantage of my patients by sermonising or quoting the Scriptures at them, there is no doubt that, as the Bible and its perspectives mould the caring relationship, there will emerge times of more specific declaration.

Craig, a final-year student of languages, was a case in point. He had come to me for counselling, and over the next couple of months or so he poured out his story of disenchantment with life, sexual experimentation and drug abuse. The God who listens and knows about human folly and degradation seemed to require me to hear Craig out, to listen to what he had to say in all its unhappy and sordid detail. After six lengthy counselling sessions, he seemed to run out of story and, turning to me, said, 'I've told you all about myself. Now, what makes you tick?' I asked him whether he really wanted to know and, as he did, suggested he make a further appointment. I had listened to him for about six hours over the weeks and I noticed that he made an appointment for only ten minutes to hear my credo! Nonetheless, I was able to tell him quite straightforwardly about the reality of Christ in my life and the sense of significance and purpose he can give. I believe it was allowing biblical principles to shape the caring relationship that won the right to be heard.

Christian Transpersonalism

In this fourth and final sector, the focus, as with secular transpersonalism (see pp. 50–51), shifts from a preoccupation with human behaviour, thinking, instincts and interrelating to a concern with what lies beyond the self. In a very real sense, all Christian approaches to counselling are transpersonalist: Christian cognitive-behavioural, analytic and personalist counsellors all stress perspectives that reach beyond the self to God, as well as the everyday human issues. However, it is in Christian transpersonalism that the relationship with God receives the highest profile, and that counselling most readily merges with spiritual direction (see figure 5).

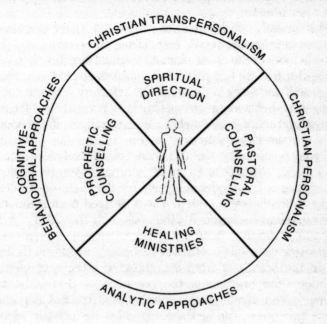

Figure 5. The four strands of pastoral caring and counselling.

Whereas the first three sectors centre, in turn, on the prophetic, the work of the healer and the 'wise', and the pastoral and paracletic, Christian transpersonalism most faithfully reflects the priestly. In terms of the discussion on pastoral care (see pp. 43–5), and, indeed, the biblical concept of the 'priesthood of all believers',[18] I would see this function, like the others, as being carried out by both ordained and lay people, where appropriately called. Even so, it is vital that those who work within Catholic and Orthodox traditions, and those who see clients from these traditions, respect the place of formal confession and absolution from an ordained minister. Where, for example, I have been seeing a Roman Catholic client and found that counselling is shifting into the realm of spiritual direction, I have encouraged the person to seek advice from his or her priest.

This 'priestly' work, whether carried out by lay or ordained, includes the 'go-between', reconciling, interceding and facilitating activity of the counsellor and spiritual director. It is within this sector that we find particular emphasis on God's reconciling and sanctifying work in the life of the believer. Whereas the aim in cognitive-behavioural counselling is to bring about changes in thought and action based on biblical perspectives, in the 'journey back' the aim is inner healing, and in 'relationship' counselling the goal is maturity. In Christian transpersonalism, on the other hand, the stress is on the journey towards wholeness and holiness. The model of change for the client or directee is always Christlikeness, whether it is derived from a Reformed or Evangelical background ('the walk with the Lord', 'growth in grace', 'pilgrim's progress'), from holiness movements or charismatic renewal ('baptism in the Spirit', 'walking in the light', 'life in the Spirit') or from a Catholic or other sacramentalist tradition ('the practice of the presence of God', 'the inner journey', 'the mystic path'). Faithfulness on this pilgrimage, as we have seen, can be encouraged by the 'priestly' element in counselling and spiritual direction, where the helper and the helped are fellow-travellers in a 'ministry of reconciliation' (see pp. 129–137). As Paul the apostle puts it:

Therefore, if anyone is in Christ, he is a new creation; the old has gone, the new has come! All this is from God, who reconciled us to himself through Christ and gave us the ministry of reconciliation: that God was reconciling the world to himself in Christ, not counting men's sins against them. And he has committed to us the message of reconciliation. (2 Cor. 5:17–19)

What are the appropriate uses of the Scriptures within this sector of pastoral care? Although counsellors and spiritual directors following this approach may find themselves handling the Bible in prescriptive, visionary and formative ways, there is here a particular emphasis on the imaginative use of the word.

There are, of course, many creative ways in which the Bible can be used. We saw, for example, the use of particularly relevant texts, in order to hear the Spirit's promptings, in the section on analytic approaches. A variant of this method, which can be a great help diagnostically, is to ask the client or directee what is his or her favourite, or least favourite, character in the Bible. If Joseph is the most liked, then it can throw a lot of light on the client's attitudes to discover, for instance, that it is the ability of the youngest in the family, Joseph, to score points off his older brothers that is so attractive! Conversely, if Ruth is disliked, then to find out that the client resents what she perceives as Ruth's compliance towards her mother-in-law may be useful in establishing the roots of the client's resentment towards older women.

There are other, stronger uses of the imagination than this simple exercise. Before considering one or two of these, let us say that by 'imagination' we mean the forming of mental images (impressions, pictures, symbols) of ideas, events, actions or beings. These images are representative of a greater reality. There is some parallel here with the fact that we are made as the image of God, representing the far greater wonder of the Godhead. If you like, we human beings are an extraordinary example of God's imagination!

Further, just as we can think distorted thoughts or foster destructive emotions, so the world of the imagination can be misused. Sadly, many Christians are nervous about the use of the imagination, seeing too readily this aspect of our being as peculiarly susceptible to dark forces. This is not to deny that there are 'spiritual forces of evil' (Eph. 6:12) abroad, but to question the inevitability of a link between the imagination and the Adversary. Some go so far as to see the creation of mental images as entirely enemy territory. Dave Hunt and T. A. McMahon have written:

Whether practised by Christians or non-Christians, visualisation is purely an occult technique offering a substitute source of power, knowledge, and healing, which, if it could be realised, would make man a god in his own right, independent of his Creator.[19]

Here is an argument which has had many parallels in Christian history. Just as excessive puritanism led many believers away from God-given creativity in the fine arts, theatre and music (and, in time, fostered the Revd Rowland Hill's concern that the Devil had 'all the good tunes') so a view that sees all 'creative visualisation' as occult is in danger of deserting a fundamentally important aspect of our created humanity. Such ideas fail to recall that, to quote Nicholai Berdyaev, 'God created the world by imagination'.[20]

This tendency by certain Christians to package the imaginative use of the mind under the label 'the occult' is aided and abetted by a modern materialism which dismisses any perspective that cannot fatten the bank balance. As Harvey Cox, the American theologian has put it:

The tight, bureaucratic and industrial society – the only model we've known since the industrial revolution – renders us incapable of experiencing the non-rational dimensions of existence. The absurd, the inspiring, the uncanny, the awesome, the terrifying, the ecstatic – none of these fits into a production- and efficiency-orientated society.[21]

With the proviso that there is a need to commit the use of the imagination to the Lord for his insight and protection, creative reflection on the Scriptures can be invaluable in the context of counselling and spiritual direction – used either during the session or as an assignment. Broadly, such techniques either carry the client, in imagination, back to scenes described in the Bible or bring the text alive in contemporary settings.

Two main influences on the former have been *The Spiritual*

Exercises of Ignatius Loyola and Carl Jung's idea of 'active imagination'. In the first of these there is a strong focus on discerning God's will through imaginative meditation on the Scriptures, since 'Man is created to love, serve and praise God'.[22] Writers like Morton Kelsey and Christopher Bryant have taken Jung's practice of imaginative dialogue[23] and applied this idea to Bible stories. Kelsey has written:

> Using the imagination we can step into the events recorded in the New Testament . . . we can participate in the eternal reality that broke through in history in the person of Jesus of Nazareth, and continues to break through whenever someone becomes truly open to the Holy Spirit. Basically, what we are asked to do is to let the images speak to us and then to share in the victory and power and allow them to show through in our outer lives in service to others.[24]

At its simplest, the journey back into a parable or incident described in the Gospels is to read and reread the account prayerfully and in stillness. Using all the senses imaginatively can help in entering into the story or situation. In the well-known tale of the Prodigal Son, told in Luke chapter fifteen, as well as visualising the young man setting out on the road to the far country and the grim sight of famine striking the land, the client might imagine something of the gnawing hunger the prodigal felt, taste the saltiness of dried lips, sense the apprehension of the return journey, feel the warmth of the father's embrace and hear the joyous sound of celebration. Within this Spirit-led meditation, the client might simply be a witness of the young man's journeyings, engaging him in imagined conversation: 'What do you expect of the far country?'; 'What is it like to come to the end of your resources?'; 'How do you feel about seeing your father again?' Or the client might explore what it was like to *be* the prodigal, the elder son or the father – thus gaining new insights into the folly of self-will, the temptation to spiritual pride or the joy of forgiving others.

Many of us find it hard to enter into the story fully in terms of first-century Palestine. Understandably, most of us lack the basic knowledge of, for example, what clothes would have been worn, what foods prepared and eaten, and what would have been the social taboos and customs of the day. And so, another method is to bring the Bible story into the present. This, too, is a longstanding technique, as is witnessed in the writings of Ludolph of Saxony, a fourteenth-century monk, on contemplating the Gospels:

> Read then of what has been done as though they were happening now. Bring before your eyes past actions as though they were present. Then you will feel how full of wisdom and delight they are.[25]

This approach also presents a challenge to the imagination, for it is not necessarily easy to enter into the mind and heart of the prodigal son, or daughter, in terms of life on the streets of a modern city, or to translate the account of the Pharisee and the tax collector into the attitudes of a cathedral priest interrupted, in the midst of saying the daily office, by the groans of a penitent but foul-smelling alcoholic. Nonetheless, a client may be greatly helped by mulling over a biblical passage until he or she can begin to visualise the realities of two thousand years ago in terms of the world of the supermarket, the unpaid mortgage, cardboard cities, the mass media and atmospheric pollution.

Kathy Galloway, in her *Imagining the Gospels*, points out that the enterprise of bringing the Bible into today's world can be more readily expressed and understood by keeping a diary, writing a story, composing a poem or painting a picture.[26] Joy and I, on a day's workshop with three other couples, have certainly experienced the way a Bible story (in our case, the episode of Jacob's encounter with the wrestling figure, described in Genesis chapter thirty-two) can speak into our everyday lives as we sculpted, painted and discussed the scene.

It is worth saying here that these methods of handling the

Bible imaginatively are not for all of us. Each of us has a distinctive personality and temperament. Some are most at home with the more cut-and-dried approach of using the text prescriptively; others prefer the reflective and visionary stance in which the Spirit speaks through the written word to bring insight and healing; yet others will accept the formative nature of much counselling, where biblical perspectives are implicit in all that is said, done, and understood.

These differences are part of our own marriage. Where I am a strongly intuitive person, Joy is someone with well-developed sensing, in which seeing, touching, tasting, smelling and hearing are vitally important in the assessment of her surroundings. Where, on visiting the home of comparative strangers, Joy will observe and be able to recall the colour of the curtains, the smells from the kitchen and the texture of the armchairs, I am likely to score poorly in these areas – although I may have become acutely aware of our host's sensitivities and the uneasy atmosphere over dinner. Because of these differences, Joy is much more at ease with the straight handling of a Bible passage than with the idea of entering into the story as if she were there herself.

At an Advent retreat we attended, she raised the matter of her difficulty over the imaginative approach with Gerard Hughes. He suggested that everyone can have access to some image of places, people and events, through which God can speak. He emphasised the value of starting with (and, perhaps, staying with!) the familiar. Someone with a more sensing temperament could close the eyes and recall a favourite corner of the house in which to picture, say, the encounter between Jesus and Mary and Martha. As an aside, it can be said that Mary, as an intuitive, would have been more likely to have valued imagining herself back into the stories of the Old Testament than her sensing and practical sister, Martha. The important point, surely, is that, whether this imaginative style is readily accessible to the client or not, the person in need meets with and is changed by the living Lord. As Kathy Galloway puts it:

. . . I have found that imagining the Gospels is not just an aid to faith, it is also a call to action. In every story, I found the questions changing, as they moved from 'what would I do?' through 'what did I do?' to 'what must I do?' Jesus does not meet us to leave us where we are, but so that we can follow him into the future.[27]

In this chapter, we have explored the rich range of ways in which the Bible can be used in the different approaches to pastoral care and counselling. As we have done this, we have been reminded that the word of God is lifeless and ineffective unless enlivened and empowered by the Holy Spirit. Each sector of counselling is not only distinguished by a particular style of using Scripture but is also marked by a distinctive aspect of the Spirit's work of transformation. In prophetic counselling, the Spirit convicts of sin through the word and enables the client to repent and live out new patterns of thought and behaviour according to biblical principles. Through the various 'journey back' methods, God's Spirit illumines Scripture to the prayerful, listening client and brings inner healing and deliverance through his gifts of wisdom, knowledge and healing. In pastoral counselling, word and Spirit join hands to prompt, persuade and shape lives through the counselling relationship, unblocking those things which hinder growth and spurring the client towards maturity. Finally, in spiritual direction, the Creator Spirit stirs the imagination as Scripture is contemplated, giving discernment and guidance on the road to Christlikeness.

Another ingredient in the variety of approaches which make up the total picture of pastoral care is that of the personalities and experiences of both counsellors and clients. We have hinted at this in this chapter for it is important to be sensitive to why people feel more at home in one sector than another. The reasons for this may, of course, be primarily theological: there is a tendency for Evangelicals to feel most at home in the sector of prophetic counselling, with its stress on the biblical text; for those linked with the charismatic and renewal movements to value particularly the sector of inner healing, with its emphasis on the Spirit's intervention; for those of a more liberal persuasion to feel more comfortable within the sector of pastoral counselling, where the focus on 'relationship' may suit views which see the human factor as central; and for Christians from the Catholic and Orthodox traditions to be most at ease with the sector of spiritual direction, with its more sacramentalist and contemplative approach. Added to these considerations, there is no doubt that certain sectors also attract certain types of personality – both for the counsellor and the client. For example, the exhortatory and admonishing elements of prophetic counselling may draw more authoritarian and directive practitioners who, in turn, may be most effective with more compliant clients. Conversely, the gentler and more affirmative style of pastoral counselling may attract counsellors who are less directive and rate listening skills highly, thus tending to gather clients who desire a greater control over their way forward.

Whether we work in pastoral or communal settings, whether as counsellors, spiritual directors or in the caring professions, let us be open to one another, seeking to understand and value the distinctiveness of those who function within other sectors. We need to see that, whatever our theological position, Church background, particular training, breadth of experience or type of personality, the Lord God can bring us all, through his Spirit and word, to healing, maturity and wholeness.

Questions for Discussion

1. Discuss the different ways of using the Bible described in this chapter – prescriptive, reflective and visionary, formative, and imaginative. Share within the group any experiences you have had of using or being on the receiving end of any of these methods. What are the strengths and weaknesses of these various approaches? Identify, if you can, the style of using the Bible most favoured by each member of the group.
2. Look at the following three case-studies (you might prefer

to tackle them at three different meetings of the group) and then discuss them, using the questions in section three below.

David

David Forrester (forty-six) was widowed three years ago when Elaine (then thirty-nine), driving back from her mother's, was killed in a head-on collision. They had only been married four years and had decided, for a variety of reasons, not to have children. David is a salesman in a firm that fits doors and window-frames. He and Elaine, both Christians, first met on a walking holiday. David's faith had always been seemingly straightforward but a prolonged period of depression following Elaine's death has left him with many unanswered questions. He has found it particularly hard to believe that God 'orders all things well' for those who love him – and, at times, is not sure whether he loves God anyway.

David's parents live a day's journey away and he sees them rarely. His mother has always been caring – though, he feels, sometimes 'smothering' – but his relationship with his father has never been good. Hugh Forrester is a chapel-going ex-miner who has always been critical of his son's physical weakness compared with David's older brother, John, who has always made fitness a priority.

This is the fifth counselling session out of an agreed initial six sessions. Although David had some counsel from his vicar soon after Elaine's death and saw his GP a number of times for antidepressants, he feels stuck with a great deal of anger about his bereavement, his father's criticisms and God's seemingly unjust ways. In an earlier session, Psalm 139 was discussed and, subsequently, used as an assignment for prayer and meditation. At the last session, David burst out angrily that if his days had been ordained of God (v. 16) then what on earth was God up to? Later in the session he quietened and began to talk about his father for the first time, in any depth. After some silence, he recalled an incident when he was about six years old, in which his father had pushed him away when he tried to join in a game with an old football with John, and said, 'This game's for big boys only!'. He still finds it hard to forgive his father.

Jane and Tricia

Jane Hunt (twenty-nine), a secretary at a building society, is single and shares a flat with Tricia (thirty-five) who is a sales rep. The two women have had a close relationship for the four years they have shared – since Tricia's divorce. Tricia, whom Jane sees as very attractive, has had a succession of men friends and has recently become engaged to another divorcee, Andrew (forty), a successful businessman.

Jane is a Christian who regularly attends the local church; Tricia is uncommitted but has shown some interest in Christianity in the past; Andrew professes to be an atheist.

Jane feels betrayed by Tricia's engagement and the potential loss of her friend. Jane would like to marry but is keen to wait for God's choice. She is beginning to fear that God might not have her on his 'future marriage-list'. Jane's mother died when she was fifteen and Jane has found herself drawn to slightly older women.

Jane loves her Bible and especially values the story of Ruth, not least because of Ruth's close relationship with her mother-in-law, Naomi. Ruth's faithfulness to God and her eventual marriage to Boaz have been an encouragement.

Jane came for counselling because of her growing doubts about God loving her. It was only at the end of the last session (the second) that the story about Tricia emerged. In discussion with the counsellor, Jane agreed to look afresh at the first chapter of Ruth by imagining herself in the role of Naomi, rather than that of Ruth.

Jack, Rosemary and Jean

Jack and Rosemary Green are longstanding Christians. Jack (fifty) works as an accountant locally; he is married to Rosemary (forty-eight) and their family – Sonia (twenty-five), married, and Mike (twenty-three), working in London – have left home. The Greens' marriage has been under stress over the last year or so.

Rosemary has found new interests through evening classes and is making new friends; she also finds Jack's company increasingly boring. Jack feels he is in a rut but, during this last year, he has been befriended by a secretary at work, Jean (thirty-eight), who was divorced three years ago. They have been seeing more and more of each other; he has not told Rosemary of this friendship but suspects that she knows.

Jack sought counselling a few weeks ago because he felt unhappy and indecisive about himself, his marriage and the future. At this stage, he does not want Rosemary involved in any counselling, though agrees this might become necessary. This is the third session. Last week his relationship with Jean was discussed and the counsellor challenged him with Matthew 19:4–6. As 'homework', he was given 'Therefore what God has joined together, let man not separate' (v. 6) to learn and urged not to date Jean before this session.

He has in fact seen her twice, feels bad about this but cannot see how he can give her up. Rosemary is away on a Summer School in Ceramics.

3. Ask the following of each case-study:
   a. Which style of using the Bible is shown?
   b. How helpful do you feel that use of the Bible will be?
   c. If you were counselling in this situation, how would you proceed with respect to the explicit or implicit use of the Bible?
4. Try to share *one thing* that has helped each of you in your meetings together as you have studied this book.

Personal Reflection

Take time to reflect on the following words, spoken by the Suffering Servant (a figure that sometimes pictures Jesus, the coming Messiah, and sometimes represents God's faithful and obedient people):

The Sovereign Lord has given me an instructed tongue, to know the word that sustains the weary. He wakens me morning by morning, wakens my ear to listen like one being taught. (Isa. 50:4)

Ask yourself how committed you are to listening to God on a regular basis. Think back over the period of reading this book and recall any times in which God seemed to challenge, rebuke, encourage or guide you in particularly clear ways. Perhaps you have little sense of God's prompting. There can be many reasons for this but they can include neglecting to give yourself the space to hear God. This can, of course, be difficult, especially if there are small children around or if you live in cramped and crowded conditions. Even so, resolve to make the needed time as and when you are able – at the bus stop, on the way to work, walking home after taking the children to school, mid-morning over a cup of coffee, during a lunch-break, by popping into the local church, last thing at night or, like the Suffering Servant, 'morning by morning'.

See, too, that by listening to God you can have an 'instructed tongue' and 'know the word that sustains the weary'. You are called to listen and to speak. Think about present relationships – with friends, family, colleagues, workmates, new acquaintances and, if appropriate, with those you pastor, counsel or direct. Are you prepared to listen to God about these people and speak his words of wisdom and comfort when you can? Then, think of others who might come to your attention in the near future – directly through everyday contacts, through your support of others who care and through the daily news.

Turn your reflections on your listening, speaking and caring for the 'weary' into prayer. You may like, finally, to pray the following:

> O Lord, so many sick, so many starving,
> so many deprived, so many sad,
> so many bitter, so many fearful.
> When I look at them

my heart fails.
When I look at You
I hope again.
Help me to help You
to reduce the world's pain
O God of infinite compassion
O ceaseless energy of love.[28]

Postscript

We should listen with the ears of God that we may speak the Word of God.

Dietrich Bonhoeffer

The whole of this book has been about listening 'with the ears of God' so that we might 'speak the word of God'. All caring and counselling that looks to the Bible is as committed to quiet observation and 'reading between the lines' as to words of comfort and advice. Wise counsel engages us in listening as well as speaking.

In chapter six, we looked at the qualities which characterise the effective counsellor: genuineness, non-possessive warmth and accurate empathy. If we needed to single out just one strand within these three cardinal qualities, it would, I suggest, be the strand of listening, a characteristic of accurate empathy (see pp. 103–106). To be a good listener, we need also to be genuine and non-possessive, since effective listening entails being true to ourselves and motivated by the best interest of the client. Yet, sadly, many Christians – even some of those in the various caring ministries – are not good listeners. They may believe they are, but often, when they appear to be attending, they are simply looking for a gap in the flow of the other's comments so that they can express their own view – even though its relevance in the conversation may be long past! Dietrich Bonhoeffer, in his description of the 'Ministry of Listening', challenges all those of us who voice too readily our opinions and advice:

> Many people are looking for an ear that will listen. They do not find it among Christians, because these Christians are talking where they should be listening. But he who can no longer listen to his brother will soon be no longer listening to God either; he will be doing nothing but prattle in the presence of God too.[1]

Bonhoeffer is right to remind us of the close link between listening to others and listening to God. Both, as we also saw in chapter six (see pp.105–106), are given high priority in the Bible. It is as we listen to God that we can listen to others 'with the ears of God', and so 'speak the Word of God.'[2]

This sequence, from listening to God to speaking his word, is brought out very powerfully in Isaiah 50:4–5. In this passage, and the subsequent verses, the Suffering Servant is speaking. The Servant may variously be seen as the promised Messiah (and much in this section speaks strongly of Christ), Israel, the people of God (held in exile by the Babylonians), or the Lord God's faithful prophet. In each of these interpretations there is a challenge for the would-be listener:

> The Sovereign Lord has given me an instructed tongue, to know the word that sustains the weary. He wakens me morning by morning, wakens my ear to listen like one being taught. The Sovereign Lord has opened my ears, and I have not been rebellious; I have not drawn back.

This is a statement of great relevance for all pastoral carers and counsellors. The faithful servant has 'an instructed tongue', knowing 'the word that sustains the weary'. Here we are in the heartland of the paracletic ministry, the call to give wise counsel to those in need, with words that encourage, comfort and sustain.

And how are we to get this right? How are we, who serve as carers, counsellors, spiritual directors or healers in pastoral or communal settings, to have and use 'an instructed tongue'? The answer is clear in the passage. For it rests with our willingness to be teachable, allowing the Lord God to waken us 'morning by morning'. Whatever the best time of the day is for us to be still and reflective in the Lord's presence, there is a deep need for regular moments of listening if we are to 'know the word that sustains the weary'. Further, the writer of these verses is clearly one who knows his Old Testament. As John Goldingay puts it, 'He has soaked himself in the words of the Torah, in the words of the prophets who lived before the exile, in the words of the Psalms'.[3] We, too, if we are to be effective counsellors, need to be people who both know the Scriptures and discern God's word for those we seek to help. Goldingay writes this of the listening prophet:

> He has to listen morning by morning. It is not, after all, so difficult to gain a general grasp of the truth, to know the Bible fairly well, to attain a fundamentally biblical theology. But to know what in particular needs to be said on a specific occasion is a very different matter . . . An authentic prophet knows what Yahweh is saying today and is willing to confront people with it. A schoolboy listens to his teacher morning by morning. So it is also in Yahweh's school. The servant listens in order that he can speak.[4]

The path of obedient listening and speaking is rarely an easy one. In fact, in the next verse of the passage, we see that the faithful servant, in obeying the Lord God, is soon in trouble:

> I offered my back to those who beat me, my cheeks to those who pulled out my beard; I did not hide my face from mocking and spitting. (Isa. 50:6)

These words seem predictive of the passion of Christ. As we

read in the Gospels, he was mocked by the soldiers who 'spat in his face and struck him with their fists' (Matt. 26:67). The passage in Isaiah refers, too, to the faithful disciple, and we can see that the close links between Christ's obedience and his suffering can be paralleled in the lives of his followers. Paul the apostle was able to connect his sufferings for the Church with what was 'still lacking in regard to Christ's afflictions' (Col. 1:24). The Christian counsellor, too, who listens carefully to God and speaks out obediently into the lives of 'the weary' will sometimes meet times of great strain.

All of those who work in counselling, where the demands of the needy can be particularly pressing, are aware of their need for inner and outer resources. This provision comes in many ways, including taking adequate breaks, going on refresher courses, accepting one's limits of time and energy, and, above all, having regular supervision – meeting up with a more experienced counsellor on a regular basis in order to share some of the burdens experienced in counselling.

These principles of support are as essential for Christian counsellors as for their secular colleagues, yet there are two other perspectives that should be kept in mind: the reality of spiritual warfare and the promise of the Lord's upholding.

We have already seen the close tie between faithful listening and speaking and a measure of suffering. Although much of the latter relates to the everyday demands of being involved in people's conflicts, frustrations and anxieties, we should also realise that, as Christian counsellors, we are caught up in the wider implications of the Church's struggle 'against the powers of this dark world and against the spiritual forces of evil in the heavenly realms' (Eph. 6:12). It is wise to be as wary of the ploys of 'the powers of this dark world' within the field of pastoral care and counselling as in any other area of Christian service. The Christian counsellor, often working long hours, needs to see that tiredness, a lack of prayerfulness and a loss of compassion for others can be used to advantage by the Enemy.

Let us conclude on a more triumphant note, taking into our call to care and counsel 'the full armour of God' (Eph. 6:11, 13). There are many elements in this armour,[5] including the support of God's truth, the protective layer of his righteousness, a readiness to move forward to share the good news in Christ and the exercise of a faith that wards off the Enemy's attacks. These are, as it were, the defensive components of our spiritual battle. There is also an item for attack in our God-given armoury, for we are to take 'the sword of the Spirit, which is the word of God' (v. 17). Once more (see p. 172), we see the call to be open both to the Bible and the Holy Spirit.

We can discern these twin elements of defence and attack – both resourced by our victorious God – in the unfolding picture of the listening servant in Isaiah 50, who, following his declaration of suffering, continues:

> Because the Sovereign Lord helps me, I will not be disgraced. Therefore I have set my face like flint, and I know I will not be put to shame. He who vindicates me is near. Who then will bring charges against me? Let us face each other! It is the Sovereign Lord who helps me. (Isa. 50:7–9)

In listening to God and speaking his wise counsel to 'the weary', we face not only the stress and strain of our calling, and, along with our brothers and sisters in Christ, the realities of battle against the Adversary, but also the promise of sustenance and eventual victory.

This path of faithful listening 'with the ears of God' and speaking 'the word of God' is hazardous – and one of its hazards is the experience of 'being put to shame' (v. 7). What do we mean, in this context, by shame? Dick Keyes has written that shame is 'a fall from ourselves'[6] in which we fail to live up to our ideals, or, we might say, God's ideals. In pastoral care and counselling, as in all branches of Christian service, there are bound to be times when we experience failure and shame. We aim high, seeking to be effective counsellors, helping our clients on the road to maturity, but somehow we miss the mark – failing to listen carefully enough to clients' stories, losing our tempers with their lack of response or giving glib advice which falls short of addressing their deepest needs.

As in all our relating to others there must be accountability. At times we will need the grace of patience as we seek to unravel the complications of our own errors of judgment; at times it may be right to be frank about our mistakes and see the resulting discussion as a point of growth in the counselling relationship; and at other times we will need the humility to apologise, admitting our fallibility and, thereby, bringing a fresh candour into the helping process. However much we fail, though, we can say, with the faithful listener, 'I know I will not be put to shame' for 'He who vindicates me is near' (vv. 7–8). Our need to repent and make amends may be pressing, but, as we return to the call of obedient listening, we can realise afresh that, though others may condemn us (vv. 8–9), it is 'the Sovereign Lord who helps [us]'. As Dick Keyes puts it:

God not only forgives, but he *accepts* us *personally*, wanting to be with us because he loves us. In all our confusion, sin, and shame God welcomes us, not out of duty, but because he loves us.[7]

As we tread the path of obedient caring we can be assured of the Lord's forgiveness and affirmation. He, the Suffering Servant, who listens and speaks faithfully, is also the Wounded Healer, the one who, though afflicted for our sins and folly, still brings healing, maturity and wholeness. We, too, faithful listeners and suffering servants, are called to be wounded healers, as we follow the example of Jesus, 'who for the joy set before him endured the cross, scorning its shame' (Heb. 12:2). As we listen to him, open to his word and his Spirit, we will be able to 'know the word that sustains the weary' and declare to our fellow-strugglers:

Who among you fears the Lord and obeys the word of his servant? Let him who walks in the dark, who has no light, trust in the name of the Lord and rely on his God. (Isa. 50:10)

Notes

Chapter 1

1 For a detailed evaluation of secular and Christian methodologies of counselling, see Roger F. Hurding *Roots & Shoots: A Guide to Counselling and Psychotherapy* (London: Hodder & Stoughton 1986).

2 Richard F. Lovelace *Dynamics of Spiritual Life: An Evangelical Theology of Renewal* (Exeter: Paternoster Press 1979) p. 219.

3 See, for example, Matthew 5:17–19; Luke 24:25–27,44; John 10:35; 1 Corinthians 10:11; 2 Timothy 3:16; Hebrews 1:1; 2 Peter 1:20–21.

4 See 1 Corinthians 12:28; Ephesians 2:20, 3:5.

5 The Association of Biblical Counsellors, founded in 1981 in the United Kingdom, aims to promote 'a biblical approach to counselling' and is affiliated to the International Association of Biblical Counselors, based in Oklahoma City. As an example of a Statement of Faith which avoids the controversial word 'inerrancy', see that of the Australian Christian Counsellors' Association which, in turn, is indebted to Scripture Union for its wording. It states:

> We believe that . . . the scriptures: are God-breathed, since their writers spoke from God as they were moved by the Holy Spirit; hence are fully trustworthy in all that they affirm; and are our highest authority for faith and life.

6 J. I. Packer 'Infallibility and Inerrancy of the Bible' in Sinclair B. Ferguson & David F. Wright (eds.) *New Dictionary of Theology* (Leicester: Inter-Varsity Press 1988) p. 337.

7   For fuller discussions on questions of infallibility and inerrancy,
    see I. Howard Marshall *Biblical Inspiration* (Hodder & Stoughton
    1982) pp. 50–72 and J. I. Packer *God has Spoken: Revelation and
    the Bible* (Hodder & Stoughton edn 1979) pp. 139–155.
8   Marshall *op. cit.* p. 9.
9   *ibid.* p. 71.
10 See, for example, G. C. Berkouwer *General Revelation* (Grand
    Rapids, Michigan: Eerdmans 1955), C. H. Pinnock 'Revela-
    tion' in *New Dictionary of Theology* pp. 585–587 and Bernard
    Ramm *Special Revelation and the Word of God* (Eerdmans 1961)
    pp. 17–18.
11 Calvin *Institutes* I vi 1.
12 Quoted in E. J. Poole-Connor *Evangelicalism in England* (Wor-
    thing: Henry E. Walter 1965) p. 38.
13 James D. Smart *The Interpretation of Scripture* (London: SCM
    1961) p. 33 in Anthony C. Thiselton *The Two Horizons* (Pater-
    noster Press 1980) p. 20.
14 See Eugene A. Nida & William D. Reyburn *Meaning Across
    Cultures* (Mary Knoll, New York: Orbis Books 1981) pp. 2–3.
15 Thiselton *op. cit.* p. xix.

Chapter 2

1   Original source mislaid.
2   Fynn *Mister God, This is Anna* (London: Collins 1974) p. 13.
3   David Clines 'A Biblical Doctrine of Man' *The Journal of the
    Christian Brethren Research Fellowship* 28 (1976) p. 24.
4   W. David Stacey *The Pauline View of Man* (London: Macmillan
    1956) p. 222 in Clines *op. cit.* p. 10.
5   Walter Brueggemann *Genesis* (Atlanta: John Knox Press 1982)
    p. 34.
6   It was Karl Barth who stressed that partnership and co-operation
    between men and women give the clearest picture of the image of
    God. As well as his *Church Dogmatics* III, 1, pp. 207–220, see G.
    C. Berkouwer *Man: The Image of God* (Grand Rapids, Michigan:
    Eerdmans 1962) pp. 72–73, Mary Hayter *The New Eve in Christ*
    (London: SPCK 1987) pp. 87–93 and Paul K. Jewett *Man as
    Male and Female* (Eerdmans 1975) pp. 49ff.

7 Brueggemann *op. cit.* p. 37.

8 Quoted in Dick Keyes *Beyond Identity: Finding Yourself in the Image and Character of God* (London: Hodder & Stoughton 1986) p. 14.

9 Brueggemann *op. cit.* pp. 48–49.

10 Brian J. Walsh & J. Richard Middleton *The Transforming Vision: Shaping a Christian World View* (Downers Grove, Illinois: Inter-Varsity Press 1984) p. 65.

11 Genesis 3:16 has been variously understood, ranging from a view that the statement is God's judgment on men and women, and therefore not to be gainsaid, to a belief that it is a prediction of woman's bid for supremacy. For helpful discussion on this verse, see Mary Hayter *The New Eve in Christ* (London: SPCK 1987) pp. 105–115.

12 Quoted in Colin Brown (ed.) *The New International Dictionary of New Testament Theology (NIDNTT)* (Exeter: Paternoster Press 1978) vol. 3 p. 1058.

13 Elaine Storkey *What's Right with Feminism* (SPCK 1985) p. 47.

14 E. M. Forster *Howard's End* (Harmondsworth: Penguin 1941) p. 58.

15 David Donnison 'The Good Society' *Third Way* Dec. 89/Jan. 90 vol. 12 no. 12 p. 29.

16 Walsh & Middleton *op. cit.* p. 62.

17 Quoted by Michael Sadgrove in *Church Times* Nov. 27 1987, reviewing Geoffrey Ahern & Grace Davie *Inner City God* (London: Hodder & Stoughton 1987).

18 Keyes *op. cit.* p. 76.

19 See, for example, Genesis 9:6 and James 3:9.

20 See also John 15:8; Romans 8:29–30; Hebrews 1:3; 1 John 3:2.

21 Account given in 'Children and Gardening' *Woman's Hour* Radio 4, 28 May 1990.

22 David G. Benner *Psychotherapy and the Spiritual Quest* (Grand Rapids, Michigan: Baker Book House 1988) p. 128.

23 See Jewett *op. cit.* pp. 142–147.

24 John Carlin 'Meeting the Natives' *The Independent Magazine* 9 June 1990 pp. 24–25.

25 Michael Walker *The God of Our Journey* (London: Marshall Pickering 1989) pp. 50–51.

26 In 'A Winter Too Many' shown on ITV, 17 October 1989.
27 Brueggemann *op. cit.* p. 18.
28 Jürgen Moltmann in Elisabeth Moltmann-Wendel & Jürgen Moltmann *Humanity in God* (London: SCM Press 1984) p. 88.
29 Used by kind permission from Thankyou Music Limited, 1 St Anne's Road, Eastbourne, East Sussex, BN21 3UN, England.

Chapter 3

1 Fynn *Mister God, This is Anna* (London: Collins 1974) p. 41.
2 See the references to Leviticus 19:18 in Matthew 5:43; 19:19; 22:39; Mark 12:31,33; Luke 10:27; Romans 13:8–10; 15:2; Galatians 5:14; and James 2:8.
3 Ulrich Falkenroth in Colin Brown (ed.) *The New International Dictionary of New Testament Theology* (Exeter: Paternoster 1975) vol. 1 p. 259.
4 See, for example, Joel 2:1; Jonah 3:7; Matthew 9:35; Mark 1:38; Luke 8:1; Acts 20:25; Romans 16:25; 1 Corinthians 15:14; 2 Corinthians 5:17; 6:2; Ephesians 5:8; 2 Timothy 4:17; and Titus 1:3.
5 See Psalms 111:10; Proverbs 1:7; Isaiah 2:3; Matthew 9:35; 28:20; Luke 21:37; John 6:59; 14:26; Acts 4:2; 15:35; Romans 12:7; 1 Corinthians 2:13; 2 Thessalonians 2:15; 2 Timothy 2:2; Hebrews 5:12.
6 For the various meanings of *parakaleo*: (a) summon, invite, ask, implore, see Matthew 26:53; Luke 7:4; Acts 16:9; 28:20; (b) exhort, see Acts 15:32; 16:40; Romans 12:8; 1 Corinthians 14:31; 2 Corinthians 6:1; Philippians 2:1; 1 Thessalonians 3:2; and (c) comfort, encourage, console, see Matthew 5:4; Romans 15:4; 2 Corinthians 1:3–7; 7:4; 1 Thessalonians 3:7; Hebrews 13:22.
7 Jacob Firet *Dynamics of Pastoring* (Grand Rapids, Michigan: Eerdmans 1986) p. 82.
8 Thomas à Kempis *The Imitation of Christ* (Harmondsworth: Penguin 1952) p. 27.
9 William A. Clebsch & Charles R. Jaekle *Pastoral Care in Historical Perspective* (New York: Jason Aronson edn 1975) p. 4.

10 For a carefully reasoned discussion of the limitations of Clebsch & Jaekle's definition, see Stephen Pattison *A Critique of Pastoral Care* (London: SCM Press 1988) pp. 11–18. Pattison, on p. 13, helpfully modifies their definition to:

> Pastoral care is that activity, undertaken especially by representative Christian persons, directed towards the elimination and relief of sin and sorrow and the presentation of all people perfect in Christ to God.

11 For helpful overviews of the story of pastoral care, see David G. Benner *Psychotherapy and the Spiritual Quest* (Grand Rapids, Michigan: Baker Book House 1988; London: Hodder & Stoughton 1989) pp. 18–27; Clebsch & Jaekle *op. cit.*; J. T. McNeill *A History of the Cure of Souls* (New York: Harper & Row 1951); Derek Tidball *Skilful Shepherds: An Introduction to Pastoral Theology* (Leicester: Inter-Varsity Press 1986) pp. 147–222.

12 For a detailed account of the rise of the secular psychologies see Roger F. Hurding *Roots & Shoots: A Guide to Counselling and Psychotherapy* (Hodder & Stoughton 1985) pp. 40–207.

13 This diagram, together with figure 3 on page 149, was first published in Roger Hurding 'Christian Counselling: an overview' *Christian Arena* (March 1986) pp. 12–16.

14 For a detailed and technical appraisal of the work of some of the leading behaviourists, see Richard Nelson-Jones *The Theory and Practice of Counselling Psychology* (London/New York: Holt, Rinehart & Winston 1982) pp. 107–141.

15 W. H. Auden 'Behaviourism' in *A Certain World*, quoted in *The Penguin Dictionary of Modern Quotations* (Penguin Books 1980) p. 23.

16 For a critique of Ellis' methodology, see Roger Hurding *Roots & Shoots: A Guide to Counselling and Psychotherapy* (London: Hodder & Stoughton 1985) pp. 181–188.

17 Books on Freud and his followers are innumerable but for a scholarly work, written by a Christian, see J. N. Isbister *Freud: An Introduction to His Life and Work* (Cambridge: Polity Press 1985); see also Paul Roazen *Freud and His Followers* (London: Allen Lane 1976).

18 See, for example, Christopher Bryant *Jung and the Christian Way* (London: Darton, Longman & Todd 1983) and Morton T. Kelsey *Christo-Psychology* (Darton, Longman & Todd 1983).

19 For an affirmative critique of Carl Rogers, see Harry A. Van Belle *Basic Intent and Therapeutic Approach of Carl R. Rogers* (Toronto: Wedge 1980); for an evaluation of 'selfism', see Paul C. Vitz *Psychology as Religion: The Cult of Self Worship* (Tring, Hertfordshire: Lion 1981).

20 Abraham H. Maslow *Toward a Psychology of Being* (Van Nostrand 1968) pp. iii–iv.

21 Thomas C. Oden 'Recovering Lost Identity' *The Journal of Pastoral Care* 1 (1980) pp. 4–18.

22 Lesslie Newbigin *Foolishness to the Greeks* (London: SPCK 1986) pp. 24–25.

23 For a detailed account of the interplay between secular psychology and pastoral care, including the important parts played by William James (1842–1910) and Anton T. Boisen (1876–1966), see chapter ten, 'Sinkers, Swimmers and Strugglers' in Hurding *op. cit.*

24 Jean Vanier *The Broken Body: Journey to Wholeness* (Darton, Longman & Todd 1988) p. 40.

Chapter 4

1 On the concept of the 'soul-friend', see Kenneth Leech *Soul Friend: A Study of Spirituality* (London: Sheldon Press 1977); also, Regis A. Duffy *A Roman Catholic Theology of Pastoral Care* (Philadelphia: Fortress Press 1983) pp. 36–37.

2 Kenneth Leech *Spirituality and Pastoral Care* (Sheldon Press 1986) p. 48.

3 Gordon Jeff *Spiritual Direction for Every Christian* (London: SPCK 1987) p. 5.

4 David G. Benner *Psychotherapy and the Spiritual Quest* (Grand Rapids, Michigan: Baker Book House 1988) p. 105.

5 Cited in Kenneth Leech *Spirituality and Pastoral Care* (Sheldon Press 1986) p. 5.

6 Benner *op. cit.* p. 107.

7 See, for example, the discussions in Carole Sutton *Psychology*

for Social Workers and Counsellors (London: Routledge & Kegan Paul 1979) pp. 28–29; Hurding *op. cit.* pp. 21–27; and Richard Nelson-Jones *The Theory and Practice of Counselling Psychology* (London/New York: Holt, Rinehart & Winston 1982) pp. 2–3. See also, the definitions given by the British Association for Counselling in their *Code of Ethics and Practice for Counsellors* (Sept. 1984).

8 For pointers to research which stresses the qualities of caring in the counselling relationship, see Sutton *op. cit.* chapter one; 'The Evaluation of Counselling: A Goal-Centred Approach' in *Counselling* no. 60 (May 1987) pp. 14–20; and Gerard Egan *The Skilled Helper* (Monterey, California: Brooks/Cole 1982) Introduction.

9 Alastair V. Campbell *Paid to Care?* (SPCK 1985) p. 50.

10 Based on the definition used by the Royal Australian and New Zealand College of Psychiatrists, quoted in G. McGrath & K. Lowson 'Assessing the Benefits of Psychotherapy: the Economic Approach' *British Journal of Psychiatry* (1987) 150, pp. 65–71.

11 For fuller accounts of the history of healing in and through the Church, see Evelyn Frost *Christian Healing* (Mowbrays 1940); Roger Hurding 'Healing' in Bernard Palmer (ed.) *Medicine and the Bible* (Paternoster Press 1986); Morton Kelsey *Healing and Christianity: In Ancient Thought and Modern Times* (SCM 1973); and Morris Maddocks *The Christian Healing Ministry* (SPCK 1981).

12 Morris Maddocks *The Christian Healing Ministry* (SPCK 1981) p. 10.

13 For fuller discussions on healing today see Hurding in Palmer *op. cit.* pp. 208–216 and *Coping with Illness* (London: Hodder & Stoughton 1988) pp. 62–75. For critiques of the phenomena of 'signs and wonders', see John Gunstone *Signs and Wonders: The Wimber Phenomenon* (London: Darton, Longman & Todd 1989) and David C. Lewis *Healing: Fiction, Fantasy or Fact?* (Hodder & Stoughton 1989).

14 R. A. Lambourne *Community, Church and Healing* (Darton, Longman & Todd 1963) p. 36.

15 Stephen Pattison *Alive and Kicking: Towards a Practical Theology of Illness and Healing* (London: SCM Press 1989) p. 102.

16 See, for example, John Hick *Evil & the God of Love* (Glasgow:

Collins 1979); Alvin C. Plantinga *God, Freedom, and Evil* (Grand Rapids, Michigan: Eerdmans 1974); Kenneth Surin *Theology & the Problem of Evil* (Oxford: Basil Blackwell 1986); and, at a more popular level, C. S. Lewis *The Problem of Pain* (London: Geoffrey Bles 1940).

17 Tom Smail 'The Love of Power and the Power of Love' *Anvil* vol. 6, no. 3, 1989, p. 232.

18 Donald Capps *Biblical Approaches to Pastoral Counseling* (Philadelphia: Westminster Press 1981) p. 87.

Chapter 5

1 Quoted in David G. Benner *Psychotherapy and the Spiritual Quest* (Grand Rapids, Michigan: Baker Book House 1988; London: Hodder & Stoughton 1989) p. 22.

2 William Shakespeare *Measure for Measure*.

3 Jerome D. Frank in Sidney Bloch (ed.) *An Introduction to the Psychotherapies* (Oxford: OUP 1979) p. 1.

4 John Goldingay *God's Prophet, God's Servant* (Exeter: Paternoster Press 1984) p. 58.

5 Jesus was widely seen as having the stamp of the true prophet; see, for example: Mark 6:15; Luke 7:16, 13:33, 24:19; John 6:14, 7:40; Acts 3:17–26, 7:37, 52–53.

6 Robert Lambourne *Community, Church and Healing* (London: Darton, Longman & Todd 1963) p. 110.

7 Quoted in J. N. Isbister *Freud: An Introduction to His Life & Work* (Cambridge: Polity Press 1985) p. 208.

8 Alastair V. Campbell *Paid to Care? The Limits of Professionalism in Pastoral Care* (London: SPCK 1985) p. 50.

9 See Seward Hiltner *Preface to Pastoral Theology* (Nashville: Abingdon Press 1958).

10 Thomas C. Oden *Pastoral Theology: Essentials of Ministry* (San Francisco: Harper & Row 1983) p. 49, quoted in Derek Tidball *Skilful Shepherds* (Leicester: IVP 1986) p. 45. See Tidball *op. cit.* pp. 14–15, 45–48, for a helpful discussion of the shepherd analogy.

11 From the Midrash and quoted in Colin Brown (ed.) *NIDNTT* vol. 3 (Paternoster Press 1978) p. 566.

12 Alastair V. Campbell *Rediscovering Pastoral Care* (London: Darton, Longman & Todd 1986) p. 33.

13 The term 'pastoral counselling' is open to confusion. Tradition-
    ally, the phrase, as part of the 'pastoral counselling movement'
    which grew up in the United States in the 1930s and 1940s,
    refers to counselling carried out by the ordained ministry.
    Secondly, the term is broadly used to denote an aspect of the
    Church's pastoral care. Thirdly, as in this instance, we can use
    the phrase 'pastoral counselling' for approaches to counselling, by
    lay or ordained Christians, which emphasise the relating qualities
    of Christ. For further discussion on the use of the term 'pastoral
    counselling', see note 12, chapter nine (p. 199).

Chapter 6

1   Quoted in Alastair Campbell *Paid to Care?* p. 36.
2   See Roger F. Hurding *Roots & Shoots: A Guide to Counsel-
    ling and Psychotherapy* (London: Hodder & Stoughton 1985)
    pp. 28–29.
3   For discussion on these 'core conditions' of effective counsel-
    ling, see: Gerard Egan *The Skilled Helper* (Monterey, Cali-
    fornia: Brooks/Cole 1982) pp. 120–147; Hurding *op. cit.* pp.
    29–36; Richard Nelson-Jones *The Theory and Practice of Coun-
    selling Psychology* (London: Holt, Rinehart & Winston 1982)
    pp. 210–243; Carole Sutton *Psychology for Social Workers and
    Counsellors* (London: Routledge & Kegan Paul 1979) pp. 41–42,
    46–61; and Charles B. Truax & Robert R. Carkhuff *Towards
    Effective Counseling and Psychotherapy: Training and Practice*
    (Chicago: Aldine 1967).
4   Egan *op. cit.* p. 127.
5   See S. Wibbing in Brown (ed.) *NIDNTT* vol. 1 p. 501.
6   Sutton *op. cit.* p. 48.
7   A. A. Milne *The House at Pooh Corner* (London: Mammoth
    1988) p. 73.
8   Egan *op. cit.* p. 120.
9   Egan *op. cit.* pp. 121–122.
10 Cited in Dick Keyes *Beyond Identity* (Hodder & Stoughton
    1984) p. 158.
11 Truax & Carkhuff *op. cit.* p. 42.
12 This story is told in Frank Lake *Clinical Theology* (London:
    Darton, Longman & Todd 1966) pp. 8–9.

13   Truax & Carkhuff *op. cit.* p. 46.
14   Thomas C. Oden *Kerygma and Counselling* (New York: Harper & Row 1978) pp. 55–56.
15   Donald Capps *Biblical Approaches to Pastoral Counseling* (Philadelphia: Westminster Press 1981) p. 87.
16   Quoted in Paul Halmos *The Faith of the Counsellors* (Constable 1965) p. 49.

Chapter 7

1   For fuller details on the influence of Eastern psychology on Western approaches to understanding and counselling others, see, for example, Stephen Annett (ed.) *The Many Ways of Being* (London: Abacus 1976); and Charles Tart (ed.) *Transpersonal Psychologies* (New York: Harper & Row 1975). For Christian critiques, see Os Guinness *The Dust of Death* (London: IVP 1973) pp. 192–231; and Mary Stewart Van Leeuwen *The Person in Psychology* (Leicester: IVP & Grand Rapids, Michigan: Eerdmans 1985) pp. 22–28.
2   Stephen Pattison *A Critique of Pastoral Care* (London: SCM 1988) p. 13.
3   David G. Benner *Psychotherapy and the Spiritual Quest* (Grand Rapids, Michigan: Baker Book House 1988; London: Hodder & Stoughton 1989) p. 108. I am indebted to this book, particularly to pp. 104–133, for much of the thinking in this section.
4   *ibid.* p. 123.
5   *ibid.* p. 133.
6   Leanne Payne *The Healing Presence* (Eastbourne: Kingsway 1989) p. 132.
7   Roger Hurding *As Trees Walking* (Exeter: Paternoster Press 1982) pp. 206–207.
8   Julian of Norwich *Revelations of Divine Love* (Harmondsworth: Penguin 1966; transl. Clifton Wolters) p. 116.
9   This quotation and version of Father Kolbe's heroism is taken from Myra Chave-Jones *Listening to Your Feelings* (Littlemore, Oxford: Lion 1989) pp. 41–42.
10   Elisabeth Moltmann-Wendel in Elisabeth Moltmann-Wendel & Jürgen Moltmann *Humanity in God* (SCM Press 1984) p. 120.

11 See Jesus' references to Leviticus 19:18 in Matthew 5:43; 19:19; 22:39; Mark 12:31; and Luke 10:27.
12 See Romans 13:9; 15:2; Galatians 5:14; James 1:25; and 2:8.
13 Augustine *Sermon* 128.5, quoted in John Halliburton *Educating Rachel* (London: SPCK 1987) p. 28.
14 Benner *op. cit.* p. 125.
15 Jean Vanier *The Broken Body* (London: Darton, Longman & Todd 1988) pp. 88–89.

Chapter 8

1 Margaret Spufford *Celebration* (Glasgow: Collins 1989) p. 60.
2 *ibid.* pp. 112–113.
3 Extract from 'Enniskillen Remembers', shown on BBC 1, 22 November 1987.
4 Lawrence J. Crabb, jr. *Understanding People: Deep Longings for Relationship* (Grand Rapids, Michigan: Zondervan 1987; Basingstoke, Hampshire, Marshall Pickering 1988) p. 151.
5 Quoted in Humphrey Carpenter *The Inklings* (George Allen & Unwin 1978) pp. 32–33.
6 See Roger Hurding *Restoring the Image* (Exeter: Paternoster Press 1980) pp. 49–71; in Kathy Keay (ed.) *Men, Women & God* (Basingstoke: Marshall Pickering 1987) pp. 295–300; and *Understanding Adolescence* (London: Hodder & Stoughton 1989) pp. 103–127, 203–210. See also James H. Olthuis *I Pledge You My Troth: A Christian View of Marriage, Family, Friendship* (New York: Harper & Row 1975) pp. 107–130.
7 Henri Nouwen *The Genesee Diary: Report from a Trappist Monastery* (New York: Doubleday & Co. 1981) p. 206.
8 James B. Nelson *The Intimate Connection: Male Sexuality, Masculine Spirituality* (Philadelphia: Westminster Press 1988) p. 65.
9 Rabindranath Tagore (1861–1941) – reference unknown.
10 Crabb *op. cit.* p. 147.
11 Gilbert K. Chesterton *St Francis of Assisi* (New York: Doubleday Image Books 1957) pp. 74–75, quoted in Nouwen *op. cit.* p. 154.
12 From Helen Merrell Lynd *On Shame and the Search for Identity* (New York: Harcourt Brace 1957) p. 147, quoted in Stephen

Pattison *A Critique of Pastoral Care* (London: SCM Press 1988) p. 182.

13 Recounted in Patrick Forbes *The Gospel of Folly* (West Sussex: Angel Press 1988) p. 66.

14 Pattison *op. cit.* pp. 143–144.

Chapter 9

1 I am indebted to Harry A. Van Belle for this observation on Rogers' upbringing: see Harry A. Van Belle *Basic Intent and Therapeutic Approach of Carl R. Rogers* (Toronto: Wedge Books 1980) pp. 8–9.

2 Stephen Pattison *A Critique of Pastoral Care* (London: SCM Press 1988) p. 117.

3 See Matthew 4:1–11.

4 For a useful outline of cognitive-behaviour counselling, see Peter Trower, Andrew Casey & Windy Dryden *Cognitive-Behavioural Counselling in Action* (London: Sage Publications 1988).

5 Described in Albert Ellis 'The Basic Clinical Theory of Rational-Emotive Therapy' in A. Ellis and R. Grieger (eds.) *Handbook of Rational-Emotive Therapy* (New York: Springer 1977). For a brief outline of Ellis' ABC model, see Trower *et al. op. cit.* pp. 3–4.

6 Quoted in Roger Hurding *Roots & Shoots: A Guide to Counselling and Psychotherapy* (London: Hodder & Stoughton 1985) pp. 305–306.

7 For a critique of Christian 'journey back' methodologies, see Hurding *op. cit.* pp. 361–386.

8 I have used the noun 'unconscious' in its Freudian sense to denote all that is hidden from the conscious mind. The word 'subconscious' is frequently used as a synonym, though, in psychoanalytic terms, the subconscious (or 'preconscious') refers to the realm just beneath consciousness, through which repressed material may rise from the unconscious, leading to so-called 'Freudian slips'.

9 For a fuller discussion of deductive and inductive reasoning, see Hurding *op. cit.* pp. 261–262.

10 Richard Lovelace *Dynamics of Spiritual Life: an Evangelical Theology of Renewal* (Exeter: Paternoster Press 1979) p. 284.

11 For further information on Tournier and Clinebell, see Hurding *op. cit.* pp. 308–333.

12 In this book, I use the term 'pastoral counselling' for that branch of pastoral care which stresses 'relationship' and the paracletic qualities of Christ. See also note 13, chapter five (p. 195) and Hurding *op. cit.* pp. 221–227.

13 See John 14:16–18,26; 15:26; 16:7–11; and 1 John 2:1, where *parakletos* is variously rendered 'Advocate', 'Helper', 'Intercessor', 'Comforter', 'Counsellor' or, simply, 'Paraclete'.

14 Colin Brown (ed.) *The New International Dictionary of New Testament Theology* vol. 1 (Exeter: Paternoster Press 1975) p. 567.

15 See Henri J. M. Nouwen *The Wounded Healer* (New York: Doubleday & Co. 1979) pp. 81–82.

16 On the links between Christ's sufferings and human affliction, see Roger Hurding *Coping with Illness* (Hodder & Stoughton 1988) pp. 89–93, 118–127.

17 I am indebted here to Donald Capps and his reference to form criticism in establishing a 'formative' method of using the Bible, particularly in allowing the forms of the psalms of lament, the proverbs and the parables to shape the counselling process. See his *Biblical Approaches to Pastoral Counseling* (Philadelphia: Westminster Press 1981).

18 See, for example, Exodus 19:6; Romans 15:16; 1 Peter 2:5,9.

19 Dave Hunt & T. A. McMahon *The Seduction of Christianity: Spiritual Discernment in the Last Days* (Eugene, Oregon: Harvest House 1987) p. 143.

20 Quoted in Leanne Payne *The Healing Presence* (Kingsway 1989) p. 66.

21 Quoted in Patrick Forbes *The Gospel of Folly* (West Sussex: Angel Press 1988) p. 93.

22 Ignatius Loyola *The Spiritual Exercises* quoted in Sheila Cassidy *Sharing the Darkness: The Spirituality of Caring* (London: Darton, Longman & Todd 1988) p. 149.

23 For a critique of Jung's 'active imagination' and the influence of Jung on Christopher Bryant and Morton Kelsey, see Hurding *op. cit.* pp. 337–360. There has been a huge revival of interest in Jung in recent years and there is a great need for Christian discernment in evaluating his theory and practice. For a strong

negative criticism of Jung's views, see Leanne Payne *The Healing Presence* (Eastbourne: Kingsway 1989) pp. 210–217; she writes:

> Jung has tapped into the demonic plane of the supernatural world, which is hostile not only to the Judeo-Christian world-view, but to all systems containing objective moral and spiritual value. Within this world the self becomes god. (pp. 211–212)

24 Morton Kelsey *The Other Side of Silence: A Guide to Christian Meditation* (London: SPCK 1977) p. 188.
25 Quoted in Kathy Galloway *Imagining the Gospels* (SPCK 1988) p. 5.
26 *ibid*. pp. 5–6.
27 *ibid*. pp. 6–7.
28 George Appleton *Prayers from a Troubled Heart* (Darton, Longman & Todd 1983) p. 50, quoted in Joyce Huggett *The Smile of Love* (Hodder & Stoughton 1990) p. 184.

Postscript

1 Dietrich Bonhoeffer *Life Together* (London: SCM Press 1954) p. 75.
2 *ibid*. p. 76.
3 John Goldingay *God's Prophet, God's Servant* (Exeter: Paternoster Press 1984) p. 134.
4 *ibid*. p. 135.
5 See Ephesians 6:10–18.
6 Dick Keyes *Beyond Identity* (London: Hodder & Stoughton 1986) p. 92.
7 *ibid*. p. 81.

Selected Bibliography

Because the subject of this book is a wide one it has been difficult to make a selection of appropriate books for further reading. Of those chosen, books of an introductory nature have been marked with an asterisk (*); many of these would be suitable for introductory courses in pastoral care and counselling. Amongst the remaining books, a number are suitable for study and could be used in more comprehensive training courses; these have been marked (†). Books that are unmarked are, on the whole, more specialist but will repay further study for those interested. The titles are given in categories which broadly match the chapters of *The Bible and Counselling*.

Understanding the Bible

G. C. Berkouwer *General Revelation* (Grand Rapids, Michigan: Eerdmans 1955).

*John Drane *Tune in to the Bible* (London: Scripture Union 1989).

†I. Howard Marshall *Biblical Inspiration* (London: Hodder & Stoughton 1982).

Eugene A. Nida & William D. Reyburn *Meaning Across Cultures* (Mary Knoll, New York: Orbis Books 1981).

†J. I. Packer *God has Spoken: Revelation and the Bible* (London: Hodder & Stoughton edn 1979).

Anthony C. Thiselton *The Two Horizons* (Exeter: Paternoster Press 1980).

Understanding Human Nature

*Anne Atkins *Split Image: Male and Female after God's Likeness* (London: Hodder & Stoughton 1987).

David J. Atkinson *The Message of Genesis 1–11* (Leicester: IVP 1990).

Henri Blocher *In the Beginning* (IVP 1984).

†Lawrence J. Crabb *Understanding People: Deep Longings for Relationship* (Grand Rapids, Michigan: Zondervan 1987; Basingstoke, Hampshire: Marshall Pickering 1988).

Mary Hayter *The New Eve in Christ* (London: SPCK 1987).

Anthony A. Hoekema *The Christian Looks at Himself* (Grand Rapids, Michigan: Eerdmans 1975).

Anthony A. Hoekema *Created in God's Image* (Eerdmans 1986).

Paul K. Jewett *Man as Male and Female* (Eerdmans 1975).

†Kathy Keay (ed.) *Men, Women & God* (Basingstoke: Marshall Pickering 1987).

†Roy McCloughry *Men and Masculinity: From Power to Love* (London: Hodder & Stoughton 1992).

†H. D. McDonald *The Christian View of Man* (London: Marshall, Morgan & Scott 1981).

*Josh McDowell *His Image My Image* (Amersham-on-the-Hill, Buckinghamshire: Scripture Press 1985).

Elisabeth Moltmann-Wendel & Jürgen Moltmann *Humanity in God* (London: SCM Press 1984).

†Mary Stewart Van Leeuwen *The Person in Psychology: A Contemporary Christian Appraisal* (IVP 1985)

†Mary Stewart Van Leeuwen *Gender and Grace: Women and Men in a Changing World* (IVP 1990).

†Elaine Storkey *What's Right with Feminism* (SPCK 1985).

Caring and Counselling

David W. Augsburger *Pastoral Counselling across Cultures* (Philadelphia: Westminster Press 1986).

†Alastair V. Campbell *Paid to Care? The Limits of Professionalism in Pastoral Care* (London: SPCK 1985).

Alastair V. Campbell *Rediscovering Pastoral Care* (London: Darton, Longman & Todd edn 1986).

Sheila Cassidy *Sharing the Darkness: The Spirituality of Caring* (Darton, Longman & Todd 1988).

Gary R. Collins *Innovative Approaches to Counselling* (Milton Keynes: Word Publishing 1987).

*Gary Collins *Can You Trust Counselling?* (Leicester: IVP 1988).

†Roger Hurding *Roots & Shoots: A Guide to Counselling and Psychotherapy* (London: Hodder & Stoughton 1985).

Michael Jacobs *Faith or Fear: A Reader in Pastoral Care and Counselling* (Darton, Longman & Todd 1987).

†Stephen Pattison *A Critique of Pastoral Care* (London: SCM Press 1988).

†Derek Tidball *Skilful Shepherds* (IVP 1986).

Robert J Wicks, Richard D. Parsons & Donald E. Capps *Clinical Handbook of Pastoral Counselling* (New York & Mahwah, New Jersey: Paulist Press 1985).

Healing and Spiritual Direction

†David G. Benner *Psychotherapy and the Spiritual Quest* (London: Hodder & Stoughton 1989).

†Rex Gardner *Healing Miracles: A Doctor Investigates* (London: Darton, Longman & Todd 1986).

John Gunstone *The Lord is Our Healer: Spiritual Renewal and the Ministry of Healing* (Hodder & Stoughton 1986).

*John Gunstone *Signs & Wonders: The Wimber Phenomenon* (Darton, Longman & Todd 1989).

*Roger Hurding *Coping with Illness* (Hodder & Stoughton 1988).

*Gordon Jeff *Spiritual Direction for Every Christian* (London: SPCK 1987).

†R. A. Lambourne *Community, Church & Healing: A Study of Some of the Corporate Aspects of the Church's Ministry to the Sick* (London: Arthur James edn 1987).

†Kenneth Leech *Soul Friend: a Study of Spirituality* (London: Sheldon Press 1977).

†Kenneth Leech *Spirituality and Pastoral Care* (Sheldon Press 1986).

David Lewis *Healing: Fiction, Fantasy or Fact?* (Hodder & Stoughton 1989).

*Anne Long *Approaches to Spiritual Direction* (Grove Books 1984).

*Frances MacNutt *Healing* (Notre Dame, Indiana: Ave Maria Press 1974).

†Morris Maddocks *The Christian Healing Ministry* (SPCK 1981).

†Stephen Pattison *Alive and Kicking: Towards a Practical Theology of Illness and Healing* (London: SCM Press 1989).

†Leanne Payne *The Healing Presence* (Eastbourne: Kingsway 1989).

*Mary Pytches *Yesterday's Child: Understanding & Healing Present Problems by Examining the Past* (London: Hodder & Stoughton 1990).

Margaret Spufford *Celebration* (Glasgow: Collins 1989).

*Flora Slosson Wuellner *Prayer, Stress, & Our Inner Wounds* (Guildford: Eagle 1991).

The Effective Carer

*Duncan Buchanan *The Counselling of Jesus* (London: Hodder & Stoughton 1985).

†Gerard Egan *The Skilled Helper: Models, Skills, and Methods for Effective Helping* (Monterey, California: Brooks/Cole Publishing Company 1990).

*Joyce Huggett *Listening to Others* (Hodder & Stoughton 1988).

*Roger Hurding *Restoring the Image: An Introduction to Christian Caring and Counselling* (Exeter: Paternoster Press 1980).

*Michael Jacob *Still Small Voice: An Introduction to Pastoral Counselling* (London: SPCK 1982).

†Eugene Kennedy *On Becoming a Counselor: A Basic Guide for Non-Professional Counselors* (New York: The Seabury Press 1977).

Philip Ledger *Counselling and the Holy Spirit* (London: Marshall Pickering 1989).

Richard Nelson-Jones *The Theory and Practice of Counselling Psychology* (London/New York: Holt, Rinehart & Winston 1982).

*Evelyn Peterson *Who Cares?: A Handbook of Christian Counselling* (Paternoster Press 1980).

Change and Growth

†Dietrich Bonhoeffer *Life Together* (London: SCM Press 1954).

*Francis Dewar *Live for a Change: Discovering & Using Your Gifts* (London: Darton, Longman & Todd 1988).

*Richard Foster *Celebration of Discipline* (London: Hodder & Stoughton 1978).

*Joyce Huggett *Listening to God* (Hodder & Stoughton 1986).

*Gerard W. Hughes *God of Surprises* (Darton, Longman & Todd 1985).

*Anne Long *Listening* (Darton, Longman & Todd 1990).

Henri Nouwen *Reaching Out* (Collins 1980).

M. Scott Peck *The Road Less Travelled* (London: Random Century 1987).

Jean Vanier *The Broken Body: Journey to Wholeness* (Darton, Longman & Todd 1988).

Michael Walker *The God of Our Journey* (London: Marshall Pickering 1989).

†David Watson *Discipleship* (Hodder & Stoughton 1981).

How to Care and Counsel

†Howard Clinebell *Basic Types of Pastoral Care and Counselling* (London: SCM Press 1984).

Gary R. Collins (ed.) *Helping People Grow: Practical Approaches to Christian Counselling* (Santa Ana, California: Vision House 1980).

†Gary R. Collins *Christian Counselling:* A Comprehensive Guide (Word Publishers, 1988).

Sheila Danow & Caroline Bailey *Developing Skills with People* (Wiley 1988).

†Gerard Egan *Exercises in Helping Skills: A Training Manual to Accompany 'The Skilled Helper'* (Monterey, California: Brooks/Cole 1985).

*Michael Jacobs *Swift to Hear: Facilitating Skills in Listening and Responding* (SPCK 1985).

Jean C. Morrison *A Tool for Christians* (Edinburgh: Department of Education edn. 1987) *A Tool for Christians Book Two* (Edinburgh: Department of Education 1983). These books are based on transactional analysis (TA).

†Richard Nelson-Jones *Practical Counselling and Helping Skills: Helping Clients to Help Themselves* (London: Cassell 1988).

Philip Priestley, James McGuire, David Flegg, Valerie Hemsley & David Welham *Social Skills and Personal Problem Solving: A Handbook of Methods* (London: Tavistock 1978).

*Philip Priestley & James McGuire *Learning to Help: Basic Skills Exercises* (London/New York: Tavistock Publications 1983).

H. Norman Wright *Self-Talk, Imagery and Prayer in Counselling* (Word Publishing 1987).

†Harry Wright *Groupwork: Perspectives and Practice* (Harrow, Middlesex: Scutari Press 1989).

Using the Bible

Jay E. Adams *Competent to Counsel* (Grand Rapids, Michigan: Baker Book House 1970).

†Donald Capps *Biblical Approaches to Pastoral Counselling* (Philadelphia: Westminster Press 1981).

*Lawrence J. Crabb *Effective Biblical Counselling* (Marshall Pickering 1985).

†Charles Elliott *Praying the Kingdom: Towards a Political Spirituality* (London: Darton, Longman & Todd 1985).

*Kathy Galloway *Imagining the Gospels* (London: SPCK 1988).

W. Harold Grant, Magdala Thompson & Thomas E. Clarke *From Image to Likeness: A Jungian Path in the Gospel Journey* (New York: Paulist Press 1983).

Thomas C. Oden *Kerygma and Counseling* (New York: Harper & Row 1978).

William B. Oglesby *Biblical Themes for Pastoral Care* (Nashville: Abingdon Press 1980).

Some Relevant Addresses

General

For a comprehensive list of national and provincial organisations related to counselling, see the annually produced *Counselling & Psychotherapy Resources Directory* (British Association for Counselling).

British Association for Counselling, 1 Regent Place, Rugby, Warwickshire, CV21 2PJ (0788 578328). Promotes and provides resources, information and discussion on counselling, encouraging high standards in counselling, training, supervision and accreditation, and representing counselling in the United Kingdom nationally and internationally.

Relate (formerly National Marriage Guidance), Herbert Gray College, Little Church Street, Rugby, CV21 3AP (0788 73241). Counselling for problems of personal relationships, principally marital. See local branches.

Richmond Fellowship for Community Mental Health, 8 Addison Road, West Kensington, London, W14 8DL (071–603 6373). Residential therapeutic communities for those recovering from mental illness and alcohol- and drug-related problems.

Samaritans, 17 Uxbridge Road, Slough, SL1 1SN (0753 32713). Offers support and befriending to the lonely, despairing and suicidal through a twenty-four-hour service; see local branches.

Terrence Higgins Trust, 52–54 Grays Inn Road, Kings Cross, London, WC1X 8LT (Office: 071–831 0330; Helpline: 071–242 1010). One-to-one counselling for people with HIV-related issues.

Westminster Pastoral Foundation, 23 Kensington Square, London, W8 5HN (071–937 6956). London and associated centres offer counselling for individuals, couples, families and groups, and extensive training programmes.

Christian Care and Counselling

Because many of the Christian counselling centres in the United Kingdom have been founded comparatively recently, some of the addresses and telephone numbers may be temporary. Where the centres offer counselling from the perspectives of faiths other than Christianity these are mentioned specifically.

Association of Biblical Counsellors, Hildenborough Ministries, Townsend Chambers, Amherst Hill, Sevenoaks, Kent, TN13 2EL (0732 460625). Training and research in biblical principles of counselling.

Association of Christian Counsellors, King's House, 175 Wokingham Road, Reading, RG6 1LU (0734 662207). Set up to offer resources and accreditation for Christian counsellors, working in pastoral and communal settings, and to encourage high standards of training in Christian counselling.

Barnabas House, Old St Clears Road, Carmarthen, Dyfed, SA32 3HH (0267 230428). A centre for counselling and caring on a daily and residential basis, as well as for training.

Bud Christian Trust, Hill House, 22 Hill Street, Corbridge, Northumbria, NE45 5AA (0434 633429). Offers a counselling and physiotherapy service, as well as a range of training courses in counselling and relational skills and in understanding the Bible.

CARA, The Basement, 178 Lancaster Road, London, W11 1QU (071–792 8299). Pastoral care and resources for people affected by AIDS and HIV-related issues, including drop-in facilities, home support and hospital visiting; also training and support for carers.

Cardiff Concern, Regal House, Gelligoer Lane, Cathais, Cardiff (0222 664410). A service offering counselling on biblical principles.

Care, 53 Romney Street, London, SW1P 3PF (071–233 0455). An organisation for caring and campaigning which provides training in counselling. Regional offices in Wales (0222 747177), Scotland (0555 894929) and Northern Ireland (0232 242019).

Caring Professionals Concern, King's House, 175 Wokingham Road, Reading, RG6 1LU (0734 662207). Work includes support for Christian professionals in caring and counselling.

Christian Caring, The Old School, 61 St Barnabas' Road, Cambridge,

CB1 2BX (0223 68264). Seeks to foster pastoral care in participating Churches through education, counselling and support.

Christian Listeners, c/o The Acorn Christian Healing Trust (see section on 'Healing and Spiritual Direction'). Exists to develop the Church's ministry of pastoral care by establishing local groups of Christians trained in listening skills. In relation to this, fosters co-operation between clergy, doctors and others in community care.

Clinical Theology Association, St Mary's House, Church Westcote, Oxford, OX7 6SF (0993 830209). Training in pastoral care and counselling, and research related to the integration of psychology, psychotherapy and the Christian faith.

Compass, 25 Hope Street, Liverpool, L1 9BQ (051–708 6688). A service, sponsored by the Merseyside and Region Churches' Ecumenical Assembly, which offers counselling (not crisis work), training and supervision.

Contact for Christ Service, Selsdon House, 212–220 Addington Road, South Croydon, CR2 8LD (081–651 6246). A service which links Christian counsellors with evangelistic work.

Cornerstone (081-997 2975). A network of Christians in London, offering professional counselling and psychotherapy, including individual, couple, family and group work.

Crossline, Church Lane, Barnstaple, EX31 1BH (0271 44844); Claremont House, St George's Road, Bolton, Greater Manchester, BL1 2BY (0204 20166); 9 Pilrig Street, Edinburgh, EH6 5AH (031–554 6140); 5 Heavitree Road, Exeter, EX1 2LD (0392 433333); New Life Christian Fellowship, George Street, Maidstone, Kent, (0622 754447); Methodist Central Hall, Eastlake Street, Plymouth, PL1 1BA (0752 666777 [twenty-four-hour telephone answering service] and 664243); 1 Belvedere Walk, Shrewsbury (0743 236424). Crisis work, one-to-one counselling, confidential telephone helplines and training.

CWR, Waverley Abbey House, Waverley Lane, Farnham, Surrey, GU9 8EP (02518 3695). Offers a wide range of training courses, specialising in residential and one-year institutes in Christian counselling and biblical studies; also includes preparation for marriage, prayer and meditation retreats and Myers-Briggs workshops – all from a biblical basis.

Dympna Centre, 60 Grove End Road, St John's Wood, London, NW8 9NH (071–286 6107). Counselling and psychotherapy for

Judaeo-Christian ministers of religion and members of religious orders and communities.

Ibstock Centre, 111 Chapel Street, Ibstock, Leicester LE6 1HG (0530 60675). Listening, counselling and spiritual direction; healing for the whole person.

Light House, 11 Belvedere Road, Earlesdon, Coventry, CV5 6PF (0203 673734). Offers counselling, prayer and instructional courses.

Listening Post, YMCA Building, Sebert Street, Kingsholm, Gloucester, GL1 3BS (0452 303820). Counselling and training.

Manna Counselling Service, 147–149 Streatham High Road, London SW16 6EG (081-769 1718). Part of the work of Streatham Baptist Church, this centre seeks to be a service to anyone in the community, offering counselling on professional lines.

Network, 10 Cotham Park, Bristol, BS6 6BU (0272 420066). A resource centre offering support for caring in the local churches, a range of training programmes and counselling; seeks an integration of a biblical theology and psychological understanding.

Oxford Christian Institute for Counselling, 11 Norham Gardens, Oxford, OX2 6PS (0865 58154). Offers support for the pastoral work of the Churches, training and counselling.

Prabhu Guptara Associates, Pineview House, 58 Ridgway Road, Farnham, GU9 8NS (0252 713643). General counselling, especially for those adjusting to new environments; cross-cultural counselling.

Raphael Centre, 100 Ashmill Street, London, NW1 6RA (071–289 7002). A counselling service primarily for the Jewish community.

REACH Merseyside, 85a Allerton Road, Liverpool, L18 2DA (051–737 2121). Offers personal and community help and support, counselling and training.

Sevenoaks Christian Counselling Service, 42 Lime Tree Walk, Sevenoaks, Kent, TN13 1YH (0732 450118). Offers help and counsel to individuals, families and other small groups, whether church-goers or not.

SCOPE (The Sheffield School of Christian Psychotherapy and Counselling), 512 Fulwood Road, Sheffield, S10 3QD (0742 307073). Offers psychotherapy to those who suffer from emotional disorders; although the spiritual dimension is seen as important, there is no attempt at indoctrination. SCOPE is centred in Sheffield with some therapists in other parts of the country.

Spurriergate Centre, c/o 21 High Petergate, York, YO1 2EN. A drop-in centre offering listening, support and prayer.

Tom Allan Centre, 23 Elmbank Street, Glasgow, G2 4PD (041–221 1535). Psychodynamic counselling and training; also back-up and consultation for ministers, laity and social workers. Management: Church of Scotland Board of Social Responsibility.

True Freedom Trust, P.O. Box 3, Upton, Wirral, Merseyside, L49 6NY (051–653 0773); P.O. Box 592, London, SE4 1EF (081–314 5735). A counselling and teaching organisation offering help for those struggling with homosexuality, lesbianism and related problems.

Vine Christian Counselling Service, 1580 Pershore Road, Stirchley, Birmingham, B30 2NH (021–458 2752). Offers counselling, training and support.

William Temple Foundation, Manchester Business School, Manchester, M16 6PB (061–273 8228). Offers resources, training programmes and research to stimulate and develop Christian caring in social contexts.

Healing and Spiritual Direction

Acorn Christian Healing Trust, Whitehill Chase, High Street, Bordon, Hampshire, GU35 OAP (0420 478121). Seeks the renewal of the Church's ministry of healing, encourages co-operation between the Church and Medicine and has founded, for example, Christian Listeners to foster listening skills within the Church.

Buckland Trust c/o Lavington House, 63 Fore Street, Cullompton, Devon EX15 1JY (0884 256647). A residential centre (Northmoor House, Dulverton), offering training, counselling, the ministry of healing and rehabilitation for a limited number of Christian ex-offenders.

Churches' Council for Health and Healing, St Marylebone Parish Church, Marylebone Road, London, NW1 5LT (071–486 9644). Seeks to provide resources for and co-ordinate the healing work of the different Christian denominations.

Ellel Grange, Ellel, Lancaster, LA2 OHN (0524 751651). A centre for training and ministry in the areas of counselling, healing and deliverance. See also Glyndley Manor.

Emmaus House, Clifton Hill, Bristol, BS8 4PD (0272 738056). A retreat centre offering a wide range of courses for spiritual and psychological growth, including workshops based on the Myers-Briggs personality typing.

Glyndley Manor, Stone Cross, Pevensey, East Sussex, BN24 5BS (0323 440440). Offers a similar facility to Ellel Grange, with which it is linked.

Guild of St Raphael, St Marylebone Church, Marylebone Road, London, NW1 5LT (071–828 6712). A world-wide fellowship of those committed to pray and work for wholeness, with particular emphasis on sacramental healing.

Harnhill Centre of Christian Healing, Harnhill Manor, nr. Cirencester, GL7 5PX (0285 850283). A centre offering teaching, counselling and ministry for healing, on a daily or residential basis.

John Young Foundation, St Mary's Mews, St Mary's Place, Stafford ST16 2AR (0785 58428). An ecumenical centre offering pastoral care, listening, resources, teaching and training for the Christian healing ministry.

London Diocesan Centre for Spiritual Direction, St Vedast's Church, 4 Foster Lane, London, EC2V 6HH (071–606 3998). Offers training for Anglicans and other Christians in spiritual direction.

London Healing Mission, 20 Dawson Place, London, W2 4TL (071–229 3641). A centre for counselling and the ministries of healing and deliverance.

National Retreat Centre, Liddon House, 24 South Audley Street, London, W1Y 5DL (071–493 3534). A resource centre providing information on training courses in the UK on spirituality and spiritual direction; publishes *The Vision*, an ecumenical journal on retreat centres.

Post Green Pastoral Centre, 56 Dorchester Road, Lytchett Minster, Poole, Dorset, BH16 6JE (0202 622510). A retreat centre for pastoral care, counselling and spiritual direction, offered on a daily or residential basis.

SPIDIR, c/o The Revd Gordon Jeff, 43 Ham Common, Richmond-upon-Thames, Surrey, TW10 7JG (081–948 0775). An informal and ecumenical network of people practising or interested in the work of spiritual direction.

St Beuno's Spiritual Exercises Centre, St Asaph, Clwyd, North Wales, LL17 0AS (0745 583444). Retreat centre offering spiritual direction based on *The Spiritual Exercises* of Ignatius Loyola.

Wholeness Through Christ, 2 Balmoral Crescent, Oswestry, Shropshire, SY11 2XG (0691 657535). Arranges retreats for the healing of the whole person and schools in 'prayer counselling' for pastoral leaders.

Marriage, Family and Relational

Beacon Foundation, 3 Grosvenor Avenue, Rhyl, Clwyd, North Wales, LL18 4HA. Research, education, counselling and support in relation to the influence of the occult on people's lives.

Cog-Wheel Trust, The Stone Yard Centre, 41b St Andrews Street, Cambridge, CB2 3AR (0223 464385). A Christian organisation offering preventative, crisis and long-term help to families, marriages and other relationships under stress.

Deo Gloria Outreach, 7 London Road, Bromley, Kent, BR1 1BY (081–460 8411: twenty-four-hour service). Christian ministry arranging counselling in relation to the cults and the occult.

Incest Crisis Line, PO Box 32, Northolt, Middlesex, UB5 4JC (081–422 5100).

London Rape Crisis Centre, PO Box 69, London, WC1X 9NJ (071–837 1600).

Men, Women & God, c/o Christian Impact, St Peter's Church, Vere Street, London, W1M 9HP (071–629 3615). Christian organisation offering resources on issues relating to the equality of women and men, and advice on sexual abuse and related matters.

Mission to Marriage, 20 Mill Street, Mildenhall, Suffolk, IP28 7DP (0638 713047). Offers training and marital counselling, according to biblical principles.

Reachout Trust, Alpha Place, Garth Road, Morden, Surrey, SM4 4LX (081–337 9716). Developing a nationwide network of training, research and counselling to help local churches with their ministry to those involved with cults and the occult.

Index of Biblical References

General Index

Names of people are shown in bold print